Diesterwegs neusprachliche Arbeitsmittel
Aids to Modern English

Practise Avoiding Mistakes

A Practice Book for Advanced Learners

Part II: Choice of Words

(Homophones, Synonyms, Prepositions, etc.)

By
HANS BRINKMANN

VERLAG MORITZ DIESTERWEG
4122 Frankfurt am Main · Berlin · München

ISBN 3-425-04122-3

1. Auflage

Gesamtherstellung: Oscar Brandstetter Druckerei KG, Wiesbaden

VORWORT

PRACTISE AVOIDING MISTAKES ist ein Übungsbuch zu dem 1966 erschienenen, 1975 in 6. Auflage vorliegenden *Lernbuch* HOW TO AVOID MISTAKES. Der Wunsch nach einem entsprechenden *Übungsbuch* wurde schon in den ersten Besprechungen des Lernbuchs geäußert und in den folgenden Jahren von vielen Seiten immer nachdrücklicher vorgebracht in der Erkenntnis, daß sich reiner Lernstoff ohne die Möglichkeit der Einübung, Festigung und Überprüfung nur schwierig – und offenbar zunehmend schwieriger – vermitteln läßt. Der Verfasser war jedoch einige Zeit durch andere Arbeiten gebunden, so daß er sich erst in den letzten Jahren intensiver der Fertigstellung des Übungsbuches widmen konnte.
PRACTISE AVOIDING MISTAKES ist wie das dazugehörige Lernbuch in erster Linie für fortgeschrittene Lernende der Sekundarstufe II (Oberstufe) bestimmt. Es wird jedoch auch am Ende der Sekundarstufe I zur systematischen Erarbeitung und vor allem auf der Hochschule zur Festigung und Wiederholung ebenso nützlich sein wie das Lernbuch, das sich inzwischen fast ein Jahrzehnt bewährt hat.
PRACTISE AVOIDING MISTAKES bietet **Übungen zu allen Bereichen der englischen Sprache,** zu **Aussprache, Schreibung, Wortwahl** und **Grammatik.** Es erscheint in 3 Teilen

Part I: **Pronunciation and Spelling,** 57 Seiten
(zu HOW TO AVOID MISTAKES §§ 1–72)
Part II: **Choice of Words,** 68 Seiten
(zu HOW TO AVOID MISTAKES §§ 73–94)
Part III: **Forms and Structures,** 132 Seiten
(zu HOW TO AVOID MISTAKES §§ 95–120)

Part I dient im Abschnitt **Pronunciation** der Förderung der Sprechfertigkeit durch Hinführung zu einer richtigen Aussprache. Die im Lernbuch aufgeführten oft falsch ausgesprochenen Wörter werden im Kontext dargeboten, wobei die am Rand beigegebene phonetische Umschrift zusätzliche Hilfe leistet. Im Kapitel 'Word stress' werden Wörter gleicher Silbenzahl aber verschiedener Betonung sowie Schwierigkeiten in der Betonung ähnlicher Wörter behandelt. Im Kapitel 'Sounds and their spelling' werden die verschiedenen Aussprachemöglichkeiten von *a, e, i, o, u; g, ch, qu, s, th* sowie *silent consonants* und wegen ihrer Ähnlichkeit schwierige Wörter geübt. – Der Abschnitt **Spelling** ist unterteilt in 'Difficult words', 'Spelling of inflected and derived forms' (final silent -e, final -y, doubling of final consonants, etc.) und 'Special problems of orthography' (capital letters, hyphen, division of words, comma).

Part II soll helfen, Fehler in der Wortwahl zu vermeiden; auf einem Gebiet, das für die Kommunikationsfähigkeit von immenser Bedeutung ist und dem im modernen Englischunterricht zu Recht ein immer größerer Platz eingeräumt wird. Im Mittelpunkt steht ein reichliches Übungsangebot zu 'Synonyms' und 'Prepositions'; behandelt werden ferner 'Homophones, homonyms, homographs' und 'Cognate, frequently confused words' verschiedener Wortarten, ebenso wie die durch ihre scheinbare Kongruenz zwischen Mutter- und Zielsprache zu falschem Gebrauch verführenden 'Misleading words' *(false friends)*.

Part III bietet Übungen zu allen wesentlichen Abschnitten der Grammatik, insbesondere zu 'Auxiliary verbs', 'Tenses' (past and perfect tenses, simple or continuous; future; reported speech), 'Conditional clauses', 'Infinitive', '-ing Forms', 'Pronouns'; ferner auch zu 'Articles', 'Gender and number', 'Adjectives and adverbs', 'Verbs and their complements', 'Conjunctions' und 'Word order'. Jede Übung beginnt nicht wie sonst vielfach üblich lediglich mit einer Arbeitsanweisung, sondern wird eingeleitet mit Beispielen zu den vorkommenden Formen und Strukturen, verbunden mit entsprechenden, in der Zielsprache formulierten Regeln und anderen notwendigen Hinweisen, Erläuterungen und Warnungen. Diese Übungsvorbereitung und -lenkung wird die Unterrichtsarbeit und auch die selbständige Arbeit des Lernenden wesentlich erleichtern und zu besseren Ergebnissen führen.

Die **Einteilung in §§** und die weitere Unterteilung durch Ziffern ist mit der im Lernbuch identisch, so daß entsprechende Abschnitte leicht aufzufinden sind. Hinsichtlich der Übungsinhalte besteht ebenfalls weitgehende Übereinstimmung, nur gelegentlich werden im Hinblick auf das gesprochene Englisch bestimmte Schwerpunkte gesetzt und weniger Wichtiges verkürzt. Phonetische Umschrift, Schreibung (Bindestrich), Regelformulierungen usw. schliessen sich an die 6. Auflage von HOW TO AVOID MISTAKES an; die Änderungen gegenüber früheren Auflagen sind jedoch geringfügig.

Alle zu übenden Wörter, Formen und Strukturen stehen grundsätzlich im **Kontext**, und zwar zunächst in kürzeren Einheiten, Sätzen bzw. Minisituationen, damit die ganze Breite einer sprachlichen Erscheinung in den wichtigsten Varianten ohne Beschränkung durch ein einheitliches Thema dargelegt werden kann. Anschließend werden sie in den größeren **situativen Zusammenhang** eines **Dialogs** oder eines **narrativen Textes** gestellt. Da die Texte jeweils mehrere sprachliche Erscheinungen erfassen, ergibt sich für den Lernenden über die bloße Wiederholung hinaus eine neue Aufgabenstellung.

Bei allen Texten kommt es nicht darauf an, Informationen anzubieten, sondern den Übungsstoff in angemessener Kürze in einen sinnvollen Zusammenhang zu bringen. Daß für einen bestimmten Übungszweck geeignete fremde Originaltexte kaum und unter dem Gesichtspunkt zielgerechter Konzentration fast gar nicht zu finden sind, braucht nicht besonders erwähnt zu werden; sie konnten nur gelegentlich als inhaltliche Basis dienen. Weil daher fast alle Texte neu zu gestalten waren, konnten auch unnötige lexikalische und andere **Schwierigkeiten vermieden** und versucht werden, eine gewisse **Motivation** durch humorvolle Situationen zu erreichen.

Da die Vermeidung von Fehlern oberstes Ziel ist, sind die Übungen ihrer Art nach vornehmlich lernsichere **Einsetz- und Umformungsübungen**. Auf Übersetzungen mit all ihren zusätzlichen Fehlerquellen wurde fast gänzlich verzichtet. Wo einzelne deutsche Wörter durch englische zu ersetzen sind, haben sie nur punktuellen Hinweischarakter. Trotzdem wird das **kontrastive Prinzip** in der Anlage der Übungen, Erläuterungen usw. immer im Auge behalten, um muttersprachlichen Interferenzen nach Möglichkeit vorzubeugen. Auch der intralingualen Interferenz wird durch Konfrontation in Minimalpaaren und weiteren Gegenüberstellungen bei bekannten Fehlerquellen weitgehend Rechnung getragen.

Das Übungsangebot sollte quantitativ sowohl für die **erste Einübung** als auch für eine **spätere Wiederholung** ausreichen. Eine **Differenzierung** der Übungen für mehr oder weniger Fortgeschrittene wird in Part II bei den Synonymen und den häufig verwechselten Wörtern, sowie in Part III hinsichtlich Schwierigkeit und Nützlichkeit durch entsprechende Kennzeichnung ermöglicht. Die **Reihenfolge** der Durchnahme der Abschnitte ist **beliebig**, in Part III besteht jedoch innerhalb der Abschnitte ein gewisser Aufbau, der die Behandlung der einleitenden Übungen bei den späteren voraussetzt.

Die Übungen sind sowohl für den **Unterricht** in der Schule als auch für die häusliche Tätigkeit geeignet. Für die Erleichterung der **selbständigen Arbeit** sind mehrere Hilfen vorhanden, vor allem die entsprechenden Abschnitte des Lernbuchs HOW TO AVOID MISTAKES zur Vorbereitung und zum Nachschlagen, ferner innerhalb des Übungsbuchs in Part I die beigegebene phonetische Umschrift, in Part II bei den Synonymen die Einteilung in *a* und *b* *sections*, in Part III die jede Übung einleitenden Beispiele und Erläuterungen, sowie ein Schlüssel für die ersten Sätze jeder Übung.

Für die sprachliche Überprüfung des Manuskripts und weitere wertvolle Hinweise ist der Verfasser seinen Kollegen Mr Bryan Garratt, Coventry, *(bei Teil I u. II)*, und Mr Oliver Gray, Bristol, z. Zt. Bremen, (bei *Teil II u. III*), zu großem Dank verpflichtet. Für trotz aller Bemühungen auftretende Mängel ist der Verfasser allein verantwortlich.

Hinweise für die Arbeit mit Part II

Der Fremdsprachenunterricht hat längst erkannt, daß grammatische Korrektheit nicht alleinigen Vorrang als Kriterium für die Akzeptabilität sprachlicher Äußerungen haben kann, sondern daß die richtige Wortwahl für das Kommunikationsverständnis oft von größerer Bedeutung ist. Besonders wichtig ist hier die Kenntnis der Synonyme. Der Lernende muß zunächst wissen, daß er den Bedeutungsbereich eines Wortes in der Zielsprache nicht mit dem eines Wortes der Muttersprache gleichsetzen darf; wer *to bring* oder *to swim* mit *bringen* und *schwimmen* gleichsetzt, wird die Wörter fälschlicherweise auch dort gebrauchen, wo nur *to take* bzw. *to float* richtig sind. *Swim/float* und *bring/take* sind daher für den Engländer überhaupt keine Synonyme d. h. bedeutungsähnliche Wörter, da sie sich in ihrem Gebrauch gegenseitig ausschließen und bei fehlerhafter Verwendung die Kommunikation erheblich beeinträchtigen. Scheinsynonyme sind jedoch nicht nur solche, bei denen der eine 'Partner' mit einem deutschen Wort kongruent zu sein scheint, wie bei *swim/float*, sondern noch viele andere wie *to remember/to remind, colour/paint, ready/finished, happiness/luck, heaven/sky, debt/fault/guilt* usw.

So schwerwiegend eine Verwechslung dieser unechten Synonyme ist, so tröstlich ist es doch, daß die großen Bedeutungsunterschiede dem Lernenden leichter zugänglich sind als die weniger großen der echten Synonyme wie z. B. *common/general/universal, special/particular/specific/peculiar* usw. Diese Wörter sind wirklich bedeutungsähnlich, d. h. ihre Bedeutungen überlagern sich mehr oder weniger, so daß gelegentlich das eine für das andere eintreten kann, es also zwei 'Möglichkeiten' gibt. Welches Wort zu bevorzugen ist, entscheidet der Sprachgebrauch.

Der Lernende muß sich mit diesen Bedeutungsüberschneidungen abfinden und erkennen, daß es in der Synonymik oft kein Entweder-Oder gibt. Um ihm aber den Einstieg zu erleichtern, sind die Übungen zu den Synonymen im vorliegenden Übungsbuch in zwei Sektionen geteilt; unter a) entspricht die Zahl der einzufügenden Wörter der Zahl der Sätze; jedes Wort ist also nur einmal und zwar an der geeignetsten Stelle einzusetzen. Alternativen sind damit durch die Art der Aufgabenstellung praktisch ausgeschlossen. Unter b) wird der Lernende vor die schwierigere Aufgabe gestellt, unter den möglichen Wörtern das geeignetste frei zu wählen und Alternativen entweder einzubeziehen oder auszuschließen.

Vorsicht ist geboten bei der Verwendung der Sätze für Tests. Entweder sind Sätze zu wählen, die keine Alternativen erlauben, oder bei der Fehlerbeurteilung bzw. -bewertung müssen Alternativen zugelassen werden.

Wenn dem Differenzierungsvorschlag (s. Anmerkung S. 16) gefolgt wird und die mit einem Kreis gekennzeichneten Nummern einem späteren Durchgang überlassen werden, ist zu berücksichtigen, daß bei den Texten und 'Jokes' unter 'Situational Practice' stellenweise Lehrerhilfe erforderlich sein wird, da der Lernende diese erst nach Übung aller Nummern selbständig bearbeiten kann.

Stark fehlerträchtig sind auch die in den übrigen Abschnitten des vorliegenden Teils behandelten Gebiete. Muttersprachliche Interferenz macht sich besonders bei den trügerischen Wörtern ('false friends', 'misleading words') bemerkbar, während sich die innersprachliche Interferenz vor allem bei den 'Cognate, frequently confused words' auswirkt. Die

Kenntnis der 'Homophones' ist auch für die Vermeidung orthographischer Fehler von Bedeutung. Ob die Präpositionen eher dem grammatischen (wie im Lernbuch) oder dem lexikalischen Bereich zugeordnet werden sollten, ist für die Praxis ohne Belang; wichtiger ist es zu wissen, daß auch bei ihnen Alternativen möglich sind.
Der Lernende sollte Lösungen nicht in die Lücken des Übungsbuches eintragen und es damit für sich oder andere in Zukunft unbrauchbar machen, sondern nebenher ein Arbeitsheft oder Arbeitsbögen anlegen, die ihm bei einem zweiten Durchgang zwar die Kontrolle ermöglichen, ihm aber nicht von vornherein wieder alle Lösungen ohne erneute Beschäftigung mit dem Lernstoff vor Augen führen.

CONTENTS

CHOICE OF WORDS

HOW TO AVOID MISTAKES §		Page
	A. Homophones, homonyms, homographs	9
73	1. Homophones	9
	Just for Fun	14
74	2. Homonyms	14
75	3. Homographs	15
76	**B. Synonyms**	16
	1. Group one: Numbers 1–20	16
	Situational practice: *Just for Fun; Forgetfulness*	20
	2. Group two: Numbers 21–40	21
	Situational practice: *Just for Fun; See a Pin and Pick it up*	25
	3. Group three: Numbers 41–60	25
	Situational practice: *Just for Fun; Mrs Bunbury's Voyage*	29
	4. Group four: Numbers 61–80	29
	Situational practice: *Just for Fun; The Opportunity*	33
	5. Group five: Numbers 81–100	34
	Situational practice: *Just for Fun; The Camel-hair Coat*	37
	C. Cognate, frequently confused words	38
77	1. Nouns	38
78	2. Adjectives	41
	3. Verbs	47
79	a) Cognate verbs	47
80	b) Special forms	48
81	c) Some verbs of special importance	48
82	d) Frequently confused verbs	49
83	4. Adverbs	50
84	**D. Misleading words ('false friends')**	51
	Situational practice: *Mr Walker's Career*	52
	E. Prepositions	53
	a) Nouns preceded by prepositions	53
86–87	1. *At*, *in* and *on* in expressions of place	53
88–89	2. *At*, *in* and *on* in expressions of time	55
90	3. Other frequently confused prepositions	56
91	4. Nouns of similar meaning preceded by the same preposition	58

HOW TO AVOID MISTAKES §		Page
92–93	**b) Verbs and adjectives followed by prepositions**	59
	1. Words followed by different prepositions	59
94	2. Words of similar meaning followed by the same preposition	63
86–94	Situational practice (Prepositions)	67

A. Homophones, Homonyms, Homographs

1. Homophones 73

Write the missing words on a worksheet. § 73 of HOW TO AVOID MISTAKES *will help you.*

1. [ɑːmz] The girl had a cat in her .... . – The old lady often gave .... to the beggar. – The barons rose in .... against the king.
2. [ai] He lost an .... in an accident. – "...., ..., sir," said the sailor to the captain. – My brother could not help him; nor could .... . – The ....s have it; Parliament has passed the bill.
3. [ˈaidl] Though he was an .... fellow, he was the .... of his parents. – It is .... to expect help from him.
4. [ˈauə] At the airport we had to wait for .... luggage for more than half an .... .
5. [bai] I'm afraid we must say good-.... now. We have to be in town .... five o'clock because we want to .... some furniture. – The ....-election was won by the Tories.
6. [bau] When MPs enter the Chamber, they .... in the direction of the Speaker's chair. – The storm broke a thick .... off the tree. – The .... is the front part of a ship.
7. [bæd] He is a .... man; he often uses .... language. – I .... them leave the house at once.
8. [ˈbærən] The titles of the members of the nobility are, in order of precedence, Duke, Marquess, Earl, Viscount, ... – The settlers made the .... land fertile.
9. [ˈberi] Do you like elder.... wine? – The dog began to .... the bone.
10. [bɛə] This tree does not .... fruit. – Children like watching the ....s in the zoo. – Don't stand with .... feet on the cold floor.
11. [beis] He spoke in a deep .... voice. – Malta was a British naval .... .
12. [biː] Would you like to .... a .... and fly from flower to flower?
13. [biːtʃ] The old .... trees stand close to the sandy .... .
14. [bluː] After the thunderstorm the wind .... gently; so we went for a sail on the .... sea.
15. [bɔːd] I have heard all his tales several times; they .... me to tears. – The joiner .... a hole through the .... .
16. [bred] We buy .... at the baker's. – Roger is a well-.... boy.
17. [breik] We worked five hours without a .... . – After the accident the driver said that there must have been something wrong with his ....s. – Take care not to .... the glass.
18. [ˈbritn] When the Romans left ...., the ancient ....s were left to themselves. – A .... is a native of Great .... .
19. [dai] It is easy to .... a white dress black. – Every man must .... .
20. [dæm] The Wilson D.... is one of the biggest in the Tennessee valley region. – You ....ed fool!
21. [diə] The park was full of .... . – My children are .... to me.
22. [diˈsent] The .... from the mountain took us five hours. – There was strong religious .... during the reign of James I.

23. [di'zə:t] You may get away with your behaviour now, but you will meet with your ....s in the long run. – The children wanted ice-cream as a ..... – Why did he .... his wife and children?

24. [dju:] The train was .... at six. – The grass was still wet with ..... – The police has to take all .... measures to avoid accidents.

25. [drɑ:ft] I can't sit in a ....; I don't want to catch a cold. – I always make a .... before I write an important letter. – He can drink half a pint of beer at one .....

26. [ɛə] He is .... to a large fortune. – Please open the window; I need some fresh .....

27. [ə'laud] No dogs .... in the park. – Read .....

28. [ə'ləun] He received .... from his bank in order to repair his house. – Please leave me .....

29. [ə'sent] A Bill becomes an Act of Parliament after the Royal A.... has been given. – The .... to the top of the mountain was rather difficult.

30. ['fɑ:ðə] My .... and I took a walk through the park. We walked .... than we had intended.

31. [faul] That was a very .... deed. – There is plenty of .... on the market.

32. [fɛə] There was not much choice on the bill of .... at our hotel. – I had hardly boarded the bus when the conductor asked for the ..... – He was not quite .... to me. – Big industrial ....s are held in several German cities every year. – The girl has .... hair. – That wasn't .... play.

33. [fə:] Women like .... coats. – I planted several .... trees round my house.

34. [fi:t] Don't put your .... on the table. – The old colonel was proud of the medals he had received for ....s of courage.

35. ['flauə] I need two pounds of .... for a cake. – A rose is a beautiful .....

36. [flɔ:] Our flat is on the third ..... – There is a .... in the bottle. – You need not sit on the .....

37. ['fɔ:məli] .... only rich people could send their children to school. – The ambassador .... acknowledged the receipt of the note.

38. [fɔ:t] There were hundreds of soldiers in the ..... They .... until they ran out of ammunition.

39. [fɔ:θ] He is the .... boy from the left. – What will the future bring .... ?

40. [gri:s] .... is needed for various moving parts of cars and engines. – They spent their holidays in .....

41. [grəun] She has .... into a beautiful young lady. – We could hear the injured man .... in the next room.

42. ['haiə] There is a farm where you can .... horses. – Ben Nevis is .... than Snowdon.

43. [hɛə] Teenagers prefer wearing their .... long. – Yesterday the farmer's dog ran after a .... but could not catch it.

44. [hə:d] I .... that many a Texas rancher owns a .... of several thousand cows.

45. [hi:l] His wound has not ....ed yet; so .... go and see a doctor tomorrow. – The thief ran off with a policeman on his ....s.

46. [hiə] Please come ....; I can't .... what you are saying.

47. [him] The organ played a solemn . . . . . – There's the vicar; can you see . . . . .
48. [həul] The . . . . city was destroyed during the war. – You should go to the dentist's. You have got a . . . . in a tooth.
49. ['həuli] The deal was . . . . satisfactory to both parties. – The Pope is called the H. . . . Father.
50. [hɔːs] He has a . . . . voice. – The Queen's . . . . was the Derby winner.
51. [in] We spent the night . . . . an old . . . . .
52. [kiː] The ship was made fast to the . . . . . – I can't get into the house. I've lost my . . . . .
53. [kɔːs] I'm sure you'll learn English in . . . . of time. – I could not laugh at their . . . . jokes. – Do you like it? Of . . . . I do.
54. [kɔːt] The thief was . . . . by the police and taken to . . . . for trial. – There is a daily report of what happens at . . . . in the *Times*.
55. [lein] If you want to turn right, you must take the right-hand . . . . . – She had . . . . in the grass for hours. – There was only a narrow . . . . between the hedges.
56. [led] The blind man was . . . . by a little girl. – . . . . is a heavy metal.
57. [lesn] I'm sure that some more attention and co-operation on your side will . . . . the difficulties of the . . . . .
58. ['mainə] That is of . . . . importance. – A friend of mine is a . . . . in Staffordshire.
59. ['mænə] They did it in the best . . . . possible. – Many of the stately . . . .s in Britain went into public ownership and are now used as colleges, hospitals, etc.
60. [meid] After breakfast, before she did the kitchen, the . . . . went upstairs and . . . . the beds.
61. [meil] You had better send the letter by air. . . . . – He has seven cousins and all of them . . . . .
62. [miːt] We buy . . . . at the butcher's. – I'll . . . . him at the station.
63. ['miːtə] The teacher explained the . . . . of the poem to the boys. – There's a man at the door; he wants to read the gas . . . . .
64. [mist] The . . . . had cleared away when we approached the harbour. – This morning I . . . . the bus.
65. [məun] The . . . .s of the dissatisfied customers could be heard throughout the whole shop. – The old lady has her grass . . . . every Saturday.
66. ['mɔːniŋ] The widow was in deep . . . . . – Every . . . . we go to school.
67. [nait] The . . . . and his men left the castle at the dead of . . . . .
68. [nʌn] My uncle has three daughters; . . . . of them is married; one of them is a . . . . .
69. [njuː] Mr Smith has a . . . . car. – I . . . . him when he was a boy.
70. [nəu] Do you . . . . Mrs Brown? . . . ., I don't.
71. [nəuz] Everybody . . . . what has made John's . . . . so red. – The . . . . have it; Parliament has not passed the bill.
72. [nɔː] The dog began to . . . . at the bone. – There was neither food . . . . drink in the cottage.
73. [nɔt] The little boy could . . . . make a . . . . .
74. [ɔː] The ship will load coal . . . . iron . . . . . – Standing at the foot of the majestic mountain, he was filled with . . . . . – There was only one . . . . in the boat.

75. [ˈɔːltə] The priest was standing in front of the ..... – This dress is too large; I must .... it.

76. [pɑːst] The .... is ....; nothing can bring it back. – Six months have .... since then.

77. [peil] She turned .... when she heard the news. – If you want to help me wash the car, please go and fetch another .... of water.

78. [pein] He cried with ..... – There is a crack in the window .....

79. [pɛə] Which do you prefer, apples or ....s? – I need a new .... of shoes.

80. [piːs] The .... conference met in Paris in 1919. – Can I have another .... of paper?

81. [piə] He ....ed into the bag though it was empty. – A lot of people were waiting on the .... when the ship approached. – A .... has a seat in the House of Lords.

82. [plein] He took the next .... for New York. – Say it in .... English. – It was difficult for the first pioneers to cross the wide ....s of Central North America. – The engineer tried to grind the surface .....

83. [pəul] A P.... is a native of Poland. – Amundsen was the first to reach the South P..... – .... means the procedure of the voting at an election. – Have you got a flag.... in your garden?

84. [pɔːz] Cats scratch themselves with their ..... – Let's have a ..... – It never rains but it .....

85. [prei] The eagle devoured its ..... – Let's .... to God for help.

86. [preiz] "I come to bury Caesar, not to .... him." – Our cat never .... on mice. – He often .... to God for help.

87. [ˈprinsəpl] The .... food of the people in East Asia is rice. – As a .... of a college he should live up to certain moral ....s.

88. [rait] Do you know any famous play.... of the time of Queen Elizabeth I? – He has no .... to do that. – I must .... a letter. – That ceremony is part of an old marriage ..... – Do you feel all ....?

89. [rein] During the .... of Queen Elizabeth England became a maritime power. – The horse did not obey the ....s. – We haven't had much .... this summer.

90. [reiz] The .... of the sun were shining through the window. – The farmers there .... horses.

91. [red] Have you .... the little .... book?

92. [riŋ] Did you hear the bell ....? – We were soaked to the skin and had to .... out our clothes. – Is that your wedding ....?

93. [rəud] Our horses were tired of jumping over hedges and fences; so we .... along the ..... – As the boat was rather heavy, we .... only for about an hour.

94. [rəuz] The pupils were sitting in three ..... – A .... is a beautiful flower. – He .... when his mother came in.

95. [rɔː] Did you hear the lions ....? – Many countries must import .... materials for their industries.

96. [said] She .... with relief when she heard the good news. – The door is on the other .... of the house.

97. [sait] I know him by ..... – That is a good .... for a new school. – If you .... a passage, don't forget quotation marks and the name of the author. – It was a sad .....

98. [saiz]	She sometimes .... with pain. – The two boxes are the same .....
99. [sʌm]	.... of the boys were unable to pay the .... of money needed for the excursion.
100. [sʌn]	The .... rises in the east. – He was the .... of a farmer.
101. [seil]	Is this house for ....? – As the weather was fine, we went for a .....
102. [sel]	The monk lives in a ..... – Does that shop .... road maps?
103. [ˈselə]	The book.... has some excellent old wine in his .....
104. [sent]	We .... the letter by airmail. – A .... is the hundredth part of a dollar. – I like the .... of roses. – Since 1956 wages have risen by more than 70 per .....
105. [siː]	From the mountain top we could .... the .... in the distance..
106. [siːm]	Ladies' stockings are ....less now. – They .... to be happy.
107. [siːn]	I've never .... a more convincing performance of that .....
108. [siːz]	Now he .... that his plan was not good. – He went over.... and made a large fortune. – He was able to .... the thief by the arm.
109. [slei]	Macbeth hired two murderers to .... Banquo. – The .... was drawn by two horses.
110. [səu]	Can you .... a button on? O yes, I think ..... – In October it is too late to .... grass.
111. [səul]	A nephew was his .... heir. – He was the life and .... of the party. – There is a hole in the .... of your new shoes.
112. [sɔː]	I .... him yesterday. – I have got a .... throat. – Prices .... from month to month. – The .... is not sharp.
113. [sɔːs]	Many Englishmen like roast lamb with mint ..... – Do you know where the Thames has its ....?
114. [sɔːt]	We .... for the key everywhere. – What .... of cake do you want?
115. [steik]	We need another strong .... for the fence. – The .... was as tough as leather. – His life was at .....
116. [stεə]	The boys were sitting on the bottom ..... – John, don't .... at that old lady.
117. [stiːl]	Knives are made of ..... – I'm sure that he tried to .... my car.
118. [taid]	At low .... the sailor .... his boat to a pole on the beach. When he came back at high ...., he saw his boat far out at sea.
119. [teil]	The fox has a long ..... – Boys like ....s of adventure.
120. [trei]	Put the cups on a ..... – Self-control is an important .... in the English character.
121. [tuː]	You want to eat .... chickens? Isn't that .... much for you?
122. [ðεə]	The Smiths are our neighbours. .... house is over .....
123. [θrəun]	Queen Elizabeth's successor on the .... was James I. – He was .... from his horse.
124. [θruː]	The boys .... stones .... the window.
125. [vein]	He played with a knife and unfortunately cut a .... in his wrist. All his efforts to staunch the blood were in .....
126. [wʌn]	.... game was .... by Bob, the other by Fred.
127. [wei]	Which is the shortest .... to the station? – How much does your luggage ....?
128. [weist]	Don't .... your time on it. – He is so fat, he has no ..... – There are large areas of .... land along the coast.

129. [weit] I can't .... any longer. – That man is twice your ..... .
130. [ˈweðə] I wonder .... he'll come in this ..... .
131. [wɛə] You'll find nails in the hard.... department on the ground floor. – She likes to .... jeans. – .... are the boys? Are they playing in the old .... house by the river?
132. [wiːk] Last .... the doctor told her that she had a .... heart.
133. [witʃ] The third .... promised Macbeth he would be king. – .... boy is your brother?
134. [wɔː] The Puritans .... their hair long. – The .... began in 1939.
135. [wɔːn] His shoes were .... out. – I must .... you not to swim out too far.
136. [wud] I .... like to go into the .... for a walk.

Just for Fun

1. [breik] Judge: "Why were you racing through town at such a speed?"
Speeding Driver: "My ....s were out of order, and I wanted to get home before I had an accident."

2. [breik] She 's such a slow typist, every time the little bell on her typewriter rings, she thinks it's time for a coffee ..... .

3. [həul] Landlady: "How do you like the room, as a ....?"
Student (looking for a room): "As a ...., it's fine. As a room, not so good."

4. [saiz] Mr Black: "Yesterday I met your brother, Mr Jones. It surprised me to see what a small man he is. He's no more than half your ....."
Mr Jones: "Yes, he's only my half brother, you know."

5. [seil] Advertisement: Bull dog for ..... Will eat anything. Very fond of children.

74

2. Homonyms

a) *Put in the correct words:* bark – bore – bowl – bowls – cape – cases – fits – founded – lean – leave – match – scale – spell.

1. After World War II, slum clearance programmes were begun on a large ..... . 2. During the 1960s several new universities were .... in England. 3. Lots of people in India cannot even have a .... of rice a day. 4. Please don't .... against the wall. 5. The carpet and the curtains don't ..... . 6. After the old witch had been killed by the young prince, the .... was broken. 7. My brother had a two months' .... last year. 8. We had a game of .... on the lawn of Balliol College. 9. I've heard all his tales several times; they .... me to death. 10. Some Indian tribes had boats made of the .... of trees. 11. The policeman was wearing a ..... . 12. My friend often suffers from .... of coughing. 13. In 1973 there were more than twenty .... of cholera in Italy.

b) *Put in the missing words.*

1. The Queen was crowned by the . . . . bishop of Canterbury in Westminster Abbey. 2. You have money in the . . . . , but you sit on a . . . . . 3. In winter English schoolboys play football, in summer they play . . . . . 4. In Cambridge there is a row of colleges side by side along the . . . . s of the River Cam. 5. If you are unable to carry your luggage yourself, call for a . . . . . 6. In a Norman church the . . . . are round, not pointed. 7. On Thanksgiving Day the Americans have their traditional feast of . . . . , ham and cranberry sauce. 8. Three feet make one . . . . . 9. Patience is a virtue, drunkenness is a . . . . . 10. They returned safe and . . . . from a journey through the eastern parts of Turkey.

c) *Translate into German.*

1. Don't *blow* out the *light;* we haven't got any *matches*, or have you got a *lighter?* 2. John and Sheila have been engaged now for four years; at last they have decided to make a *match* of it. 3. Moles are animals that *bore* their way under the *ground.* 4. That tree *bore* quite a lot of fruit last year. 5. Will you please *light* the candle; there's nothing else to *lighten* the darkness of the cellar. 6. As *grave* as a judge; as *light* as a feather; as *tender* as a chicken. 7. For years prices have been *tending* upwards. 8. The ship is *bound* for the *Cape* (of Good Hope). 9. The tiger *bounded* from *rock* to *rock.* 10. Though he is the manager of a big company, his ambition is beyond all *bounds.* 11. The little girl got a *rocking* horse as a birthday *present.* 12. The *Vice* Chancellor and several university professors were *present* at the *ball.* 13. With a *stern* face Mr Green gave his *stepson* a *box* on the ear because the boy had *soiled* his new suit and had been rather *mean* to his little sister. 14. Early in the morning General Lee's troops made a *counter*attack upon the Yankees and put them to *flight.* 15. Flour is *finely ground* grain, whereas *meal* is *ground* coarsely. 16. After a long *march* the two runaways *found* some hours of *rest* in an old *shed* belonging to a deserted gold *mine.* 17. The ex-soldier got a *post* as a *porter* in a six-*storey* building. In the evening he had to *tend* some machines. 18. In the second *race* Bryan was the first to reach the winning *post.* 19. Though my room is in the *rear* of the *house* and looks out onto a *yard* full of old *tires,* I have got to pay a high *rent.* 20. *Crickets* chirp; dogs *bark; swallows* twitter.

d) *Try to understand the following proverbs and explain them in your own words.*

1. As you make your bed you must *lie* on it. 2. Ask no questions and you'll hear no *lies.* 3. Truth *lies* at the bottom of a *well.* 4. If you want a thing *well* done, do it yourself. 5. We never *miss* the water till the *well* runs dry. 6. *Might* is right. 7. The end justifies the *means.* 8. The first *blow* is half the battle. 9. There will be sleeping enough in the *grave.* 10. We must take the fat with the *lean.* 11. Every shoe does not *fit* any foot.

e) *Just for Fun*

1. Judge: "Why did you park in that no-parking zone?"
   Driver: "Well, the sign said '*Fine* for Parking'."

2. Mr Green: "So Brown is dead. Did he *leave* his wife much?"
   Mr Black: "Nearly every night."

3. Homographs 75

a) *Put in the correct words and read aloud.*
(bows – conjure – desert – invalid – lead – live – mankind – minute – tear – wind – wound)

1. She came at seven o'clock to the . . . . . 2. The watch has stopped though I . . . . it up an hour ago. 3. Please don't . . . . pages out of that magazine. 4. The cheque was . . . . ; there was no signature on it. 5. I . . . . you to help me as soon as possible. 6. There are large areas of . . . . in Africa. 7. Where do your parents . . . . ? 8. Robin Hood's men were armed with . . . . and arrows. 9. Mr Pritchard will . . . . the expedition. 10. In former times the plague was one of the greatest scourges of . . . . . 11. The . . . . blew my hat off.

b) *Read aloud and translate into German.*

1. Chelsea Royal Hospital was founded about 300 years ago for old and *invalid* soldiers. 2. Nowadays womankind is as interested in technical problems as *mankind.* 3. The engineer was able to explain the working of the machine in *minute* detail. 4. Her eyes filled with *tears* when she saw that she had torn her new dress on a nail. 5. A small road *winds* up the hill to our house. 6. The soldier was *wounded.* 7. He *deserted* his family some years ago. 8. *Lead* is a heavy metal. 9. At first we thought that we had found a snake skin; but soon we saw that it was a *live* snake. 10. The conjuror was able to *conjure* rabbits out of a top hat. 11. She is a *cleanly* woman; she does her housework very *cleanly.* 12. The young lieutenant made a low *bow* to the lady. 13. You may not be punished for your wickedness now, but you are bound to meet with your *deserts* later.

76

B. Synonyms*

The following exercises are divided into two sections. In section **a)** each word of the row of synonyms should be used only once, i.e. a number of words has to be put into a corresponding number of sentences (see below **1. a)**); in section **b)** the number of words to be put in does not correspond with the number of sentences and each synonym might have to be used several times.

Note: In section a) the setting of the task does, in general, not allow any alternatives.
In section **b)** alternatives are possible. (See p. 5.)

Put in the correct or most appropriate synonyms.

1. Group One: Numbers 1–20

○ **1. common – general – universal**

a) 1. In Britain a *general* election is held every five years. 2. It is a *common* error to think that travelling by air is more dangerous than travelling by car. 3. There is *universal* suffrage in England; all people over 18 years of age have the right to vote.

b) 1. A . . . . rule does not permit any exceptions, whereas a . . . . rule refers only to the majority of cases. 2. It is . . . . knowledge that she is older than she pretends to be. 3. For this post some . . . . knowledge of the most important subjects is a necessity. 4. The disappointment over the failure of the peace talks was . . . . . 5. In . . . ., English children must go to school at the age of five. 6. It is . . . .ly known that for some time France did not want Britain to join the . . . . Market.

---

*) Out of the 100 numbers of synonyms given in this book 50 are marked with a ○. This division is meant as a rough guide to their degree of difficulty or usefulness. It is recommended that students should begin with the unmarked numbers and resume the numbers with ○ later as more advanced learners.

2. old – aged – elderly – ancient – antique – old-fashioned

a) 1. He is very much interested in .... history. 2. What an .... hat you are wearing. 3. Is she as .... as her husband? 4. Sir John is an .... man now; he must be over eighty. 5. My only travelling companion was an .... lady. 6. You can see a lot of .... furniture in the museum.

b) 1. The remains of an .... vase were found in an excavation. 2. Sir John has a son, ... fifty, who is a successful lawyer. 3. A twelve-year- .... boy. 4. Does he study modern or .... languages? 5. The .... house must be pulled down.

○ **3. to change – to alter – to modify – to vary**

a) 1. The coat is a little too large; it must be ....ed. 2. The doctor told him not to eat too much meat; he must .... his diet. 3. Times have ....ed very much. 4. The next edition of the book will be slightly ....ed.

b) 1. Send the letter as it is; not a word must be ....ed. 2. The wind has ....ed. 3. If some items can be ....ed, they will probably sign the contract. 4. The sheriff and his men had to .... their horses three times. 5. He tried hard but with ....ing success. 6. Of course that ....s the case.

4. work – labour – toil – task – job

a) 1. Child .... was one of the worst effects of the Industrial Revolution. 2. He knows his ..... 3. The buses are full of people going to ..... 4. I don't think that the .... is too difficult for you. 5. His life was full of .... and trouble.

b) 1. One of the principal functions of the Employment Exchanges is to help employees find the .... best suited to them. 2. 'I have nothing to offer but blood, ..., tears and sweat.' *(Winston Churchill, 1940)* 3. He undertook the .... of collecting the money needed for the expedition. 4. He has lost his ...., he is out of .... now. 5. He was sentenced to five years imprisonment with hard ..... 6. Jack, please do your home.... now. 7. Do you know any of the ....s of Hercules?

5. both – the two – either – neither

a) 1. The boat overturned between .... bridges. 2. This picture is as bad as that one; I like .... of them. 3. He lost .... legs in an accident. 4. There were mountains on .... side of the river.

b) 1. In .... case you must help him. 2. John had two sisters; .... died in the same year. Though .... of them were teachers, ... were very different. 3. You may go by .... road. 4. Which of .... books do you want? – I'll take them .....

○ **6. occupation – vocation – calling – trade – profession**

a) 1. My grandfather was a joiner by ..... 2. If he feels no .... for the study of medicine, he will never be a good doctor. 3. What is your ....? 4. She has no .... for teaching. 5. He is a lawyer by .....

b) 1. He has missed his ..... 2. His clothes at once betrayed his ..... 3. He wants to be a doctor or a lawyer; in any case he wants to enter one of the learned ....s. 4. Every man should learn a .....

○ **7. special – especial – particular – specific – peculiar – singular – separate**

a) 1. It was a .... opportunity to interview the famous artist. 2. The old lion must be kept in a .... cage. 3. He lacks the .... qualities needed for such a high position. 4. I have nothing .... to do tonight. 5. This word has a .... meaning here. 6. The cake has a .... taste. 7. Mrs Brown's husband dislikes washing up, ...ly on Sundays.

b) 1. The *Times* sent a .... correspondent to report on the flood disaster. 2. He needs a .... remedy for that .... disease. 3. Each case must be considered ....ly. 4. His grandmother has always been a little ..... 5. We had a talk about politics in general, but in .... about the latest crisis. 6. We came here ....ly to see you.

8. to visit – to go (come) to see, to call on – to attend (to go to) – to frequent – to haunt
a) 1. I'll .... you as soon as possible, perhaps tomorrow. 2. The Swan is a much ....ed hotel in the Lake District. 3. If we had had time, we would have ....ed Westminster Abbey. 4. The old castle is said to be ....ed by a phantom. 5. The meeting was poorly ....ed.
b) 1. My cousin .... a College of Education in Scotland; her parents often .... her there *(present tense)*. 2. The youth hostel in Glen Brittle on the Isle of Skye is mostly ....ed by mountaineers who want to climb the Cuillin Mountains. 3. Mary lives not far from here; let's .... her for an hour or two. 4. When John .... his uncle in America, he .... a senior high school in Atlanta *(past tense)*.

°**9. motion – movement**
a) 1. When the big engine was set in ...., one could not hear one's own voice. 2. I ran into the garden because I had seen a .... among the bushes.
b) When the thief made a .... in the direction of the horse, the sheriff reached for his gun. 2. The Oxford .... wanted to restore to the Anglican Church many of the things that were truly Roman Catholic. 3. The train was already in .... when he jumped in.

°**10. to ask – to beg – to request – to entreat (to beseech) – to trouble**
a) 1. Don't drive too fast; I .... you. 2. The old man ....ed the soldier for his life. 3. Readers are kindly ....ed to restore the books to their shelves. 4. May I .... you for a light? 5. May I .... you to hand me the sugar?
b) The accused ....ed the judge for mercy. 2. I .... you to speak the truth. 3. The policeman ....ed the foreigner to show his passport. 4. Passengers are ....ed to fill in their landing cards.

11. to stay – to remain
a) 1. I was forced to fly home from Jersey; my car ....ed on the island until I could take it back to London. 2. I'm in a hurry, I've no time to .....
b) Why did you .... away from school? 2. Please .... sitting when I come in. 3. My uncle ....ed a poor man all his life. 4. She has caught a cold and has to .... in for some days.

12. ground – soil – bottom – floor – loft
a) 1. Some plants do not grow in sandy ..... 2. Please take the suitcases back to the ....; we don't need them until next summer. 3. After the hardships of their voyage, the Pilgrim Fathers were happy to be on firm .... again. 4. A lot of good ships lie at the .... of the sea. 5. I've just found a dime on the .... under the carpet.
b) 1. The poor people were digging some edible roots out of the ..... 2. We've got a wooden .... in our sitting room. 3. The farmers tried to make the barren .... fertile by spreading water over it. 4. He found some gold coins at the .... of the box.

13. to want – to need – to require – to take – to use
a) 1. You look pale; you .... more fresh air. 2. It usually ....s Mother an hour to clean the kitchen. 3. Do you often .... your typewriter? 4. Children .... a lot of sleep. 5. The situation there ....s my appearance.
b) 1. You .... not help me now. 2. May I .... your lawn mower? 3. How many hours does

it .... to cross the lake? 4. I .... a hammer. – What do you want to .... it for? 5. I .... some more hot water. 6. The fence ....s painting. 7. I .... my bike to ride to school.

14. to bring – to fetch – to take – to carry – (to put)
a) 1. Let's .... these books back to the library. 2. .... me some hot water, please. 3. Please .... me a cup of coffee from the kitchen. 4. The children must be .... to bed now. 5. .... the armchair into Grandfather's room.
b) 1. I've got to .... my children to the seaside tomorrow. 2. Let's have our breakfast .... into my room *(past participle)*. 3. Will you please .... this trunk upstairs. 4. (Father to son): "You should .... your girlfriend home, but not always .... her home with you." 5. Shall I .... your umbrella from the cloakroom? 6. I must .... the watch to a shop to have it repaired.

° **15. box – tin**
a) 1. I could offer you some peaches if I only had a .... opener. 2. The girl had some coins and a pound note in her money .... .
b) 1. There was not a single match left in the .... . 2. You can buy cigarettes in packets but also in ....s.

° **16. only – sole – single – unique**
a) 1. He was so exhausted that he was unable to say a .... word. 2. Such a work of art is .... in its kind. 3. This is the .... example I could find. 4. Dixon and Edwards have the .... right of printing that book.
b) 1. Laura was the .... one who failed the examination. 2. The climbing of the Matterhorn was a .... experience. 3. Our friends have lost their .... child. 4. Misfortunes never come .... *(adverb)*. 5. That was the .... thing we could do.

17. to excuse – to apologize
a) 1. He does not know how to behave; he always forgets to .... . 2. He who ....s himself accuses himself.
b) 1. The clerk ....ed to the chairman for his delay. 2. I cannot .... his laziness. 3. Nothing can .... such impertinence.

° **18. event – occurrence – incident – accident**
a) 1. A trifling .... sometimes has serious consequences. 2. The defeat of the Armada was one of the great ....s in history. 3. Bombing and shooting were daily ....s in Belfast in 1972. 4. It happened purely by .... .
b) 1. A detailed list of ....s of interest to visitors is published every month by the British Tourist Authority. 2. Many motor....s take place in the streets every day. 3. In her letter she told me of a funny .... that had happened on her wedding day.

19. to remind – to remember – to recollect
a) 1. Whenever I see that photo, I .... my grandfather. 2. Whenever I see that photo, it .... me of my grandfather. 3. I simply cannot .... his name.
b) 1. Please .... me to write the letter as soon as possible. 2. Please .... to take the books back to the library. 3. I must .... to write the letter as soon as possible. 4. Please .... him to take the books to the library. 5. I must try to .... what he said. 6. We often .... the pleasant holiday we had at the seaside last year. 7. May I .... you of your appointment? – Oh, don't worry, I .... it well. 8. .... when to go to bed, and .... Daddy to do the washing-up. 9. (Title of a book:) London, a picture book to .... her by. 10. I can't ....

whether it was on the 17th or the 27th. 11. Our tenants never .... to pay their rent. We must always .... them.

20. to explain – to interpret – to account for – to declare

a) 1. He is 81; that .... his forgetfulness. 2. The mechanic ....ed to me how the engine worked. 3. The boy ....ed that he had not found the ten-pound note. 4. There are some passages in Hamlet that are difficult to .... .

b) 1. The teacher ....ed to us why the thirteen American colonies had ....ed themselves independent. 2. There is no reason to .... his words as a threat. 3. The two boys could not .... the strange similarity between their test papers. 4. Can you .... what it means? 5. Two days after the German army had attacked Poland, Britain and France ....ed war upon Germany.

Situational Practice (1–20)

Just for Fun

1. Father (to son): "You'd better wash your hands before sitting down at the table."
Son: ".... *(beide)*?"
Father, after some consideration: "No, just one, son. I want to see how you do it."

2. A ship's steward, who had dropped his captain's teapot into the sea when cleaning it, said to the captain: "Sir, can one say that a thing is lost if one knows where it is?"
"No, you fool," answered the captain. "If you know where a thing is, it cannot be lost."
"Well, Captain, I've not lost your silver teapot. I know it's at the .... *(Boden)* of the sea."

3. Lady Bracknell: "Mary, you were entertaining a man in the kitchen last night. I don't like that."
Maid: "Nor do I, madam, but you were ....ing *(gebrauchen, benutzen)* the drawing room."

4. Man, meeting his tailor in the street: "Oh, I .... *(erinnere mich)* that I haven't paid your bill yet. Why didn't you .... *(erinnern)* me of it?"
Tailor: "I never .... *(erinnere)* a gentleman."
Man: "Then what do you do if he doesn't pay?"
Tailor: "Well, after some time I no longer consider him a gentleman, and then I .... *(erinnere)* him."

5. Grocer: "Can't you sell me all the pears and peaches you'll get this summer?"
Farmer: "I'm sorry, I can't. We eat what we *can*, and what we *can't* we *can*."

Forgetfulness

The other day, Mr Huddleston, an .... *(älterer)* gentleman, wanted to .... *(besuchen)* his .... *(beiden)* brothers in the country and .... *(bleiben)* there for a couple of days. Mr Huddleston was a lawyer by .... *(Beruf)* though not a very successful one because of his extraordinary forgetfulness. His .... *(einziger)* son .... *(brachte)* him and his .... *(beiden)* suitcases to the station and bought a ticket for him.
Some minutes after the train had started, the ticket inspector came into the compartment and .... *(bat)* for the ticket. Mr Huddleston searched all his pockets and .... *(beide)* suitcases; then he looked for it on the .... *(Boden)*, but could not find it. When he ....

(sich entschuldigte) for his misfortune, the ticket inspector told him not to worry; in case the ticket did not turn up, he would have to buy another. Mr Huddleston, however, ... *(erklärte)* to him why he so urgently .... *(brauchte)* the ticket: "It's a problem of .... *(besonderer)* importance to me; I don't .... *(erinnere mich)* where to get out."

2. Group Two: Numbers 21–40

○ **21. serious – grave – earnest**

a) 1. If prices do not stop rising, the government will have to take .... measures. 2. She did not do the examination in spite of my .... advice. 3. Are you really .... when you say that you don't want to help me?
b) 1. The situation in the Near East is growing more and more ..... 2. We ....ly hope that he is not ....ly ill. 3. We have .... doubts as to whether his intentions are .....

○ **22. factory – mill – works – plant**

a) 1. Most of the cotton .... are located in northern England with Manchester as the commercial centre. 2. The gas.... is near the station. 3. On our arrival we were shown around the ..... 4. The .... workers have been on strike now for two weeks.
b) 1. Pittsburgh is a big industrial city with several steel..... 2. Under the .... Act of 1833 children were not allowed to work longer than 48 hours a week. 3. As the area is rich in forests, you'll find a lot of saw ....s there.

23. to go – to travel – to run – to ride – to drive – to sail

a) 1. We prefer ....ing in a train to ....ing in a bus. 2. Do you want to .... by bus or by train? 3. How often does the bus ....? 4. The ship is ....ing for Bombay. 5. I'd like to .... round the world. 6. At a ....ing school you can learn how to .... a car.
b) 1. That young man ....s rather carelessly. 2. When are you ....ing to Oxford? 3. He was .... over by a bus. 4. Can you .... a motorcycle? 5. Last summer we .... thousands of miles through Canada. 6. Trams don't .... here any longer. 7. Let's .... on the upper deck of the bus. 8. Shall we walk or ....? My car's in the garage.

○ **24. wrong – false**

a) 1. The dentist fitted him a new set of .... teeth. 2. You've taken the .... key.
b) 1. He always does the .... thing. 2. The ship sailed under .... colours. 3. My watch is ..... 4. Everything went .... at the meeting. 5. The street hawker used .... weights.

25. colour – paint – dye – complexion

a) 1. I want some brown .... for my garden gate. 2. What .... is your new car? 3. The sunlight has faded the curtains; you should wash them in blue ..... 4. Mrs Micawber had a young woman of dark .... as a servant.
b) 1. The .... of her hair does not agree with her ....; perhaps she used too much ..... 2. Does the painter prefer oil-bound or water-bound ....s? 3. I'm afraid you are ....-blind. 4. It's the weather side; you must give the wall at least three coats of ..... 5. The magician painted the mask with his magic ....s.

26. mistake – error – blunder – fault – defect

a) 1. He has got a bodily ....; please pretend not to see it. 2. There are some ....s in your invoice. 3. I'm afraid he'll make an awful .... in marrying her. 4. There are only some slight ....s in your translation. 5. People see the ....s of others sooner than their own.

b) 1. With all her . . . .s she was a good wife to him. 2. There must be some . . . . ; this is not a ticket to Reading. 3. The management made a fatal . . . . in ignoring the legitimate demands of the workers. 4. It was my . . . . that the . . . . in your car could not be repaired sooner.

27. ready – finished

a) 1. After that performance he is . . . . as an actor. 2. But he is not . . . . to give up acting yet.
b) 1. The hotel was completely . . . . and . . . . to receive the first guests when it was destroyed by fire. 2. Have the boys . . . . their homework? 3. Is everything . . . . for the party? 4. The packers placed the . . . . articles into crates for export. 5. Have you . . . . reading? 6. Get the room . . . . for the meeting.

○ **28. flesh – meat**

a) 1. It is nothing serious; it is only a . . . . wound. 2. While my wife was on holiday, I had to eat tinned . . . . all the time.
b) 1. The soup was excellent, especially the little . . . . balls in it. 2. O God; that bread should be so dear, and . . . . and blood so cheap! *(Thomas Hood, Song of the Shirt)* 3. She likes to wear . . . .-coloured stockings.

29.1 woman – wife – lady – madam – Mrs – mistress

a) 1. What can I do for you, ... ? 2. . . . . Brown is a real . . . . . 3. Mr Green will come with his . . . . . 4. A married . . . . should know how to boil eggs. 5. Commercial traveller to servant: "Can I see the . . . . of the house?"
b) 1. Who is the . . . . over there? – She is Lord Cunningham's . . . . . 2. He left his . . . . and children to go to South America. 3. Today there are no longer separate compartments for . . . .s.

29.2 man – husband – gentleman – sir – Mr – master

a) 1. One can't serve two . . . .s. 2. He does not behave like a . . . . . 3. Do you know . . . . Smith? – Yes, ... 4. Mrs White lives all by herself; her . . . . died last year. 5. He is the right . . . . in the right place.
b) 1. Please remember me to your . . . . , Mrs Lee. 2. Like . . . . , like . . . . . 3. It is almost a definition of a . . . . to say that he is one who never inflicts pain. *(J. H. Newman)* 4. Who is that . . . . ? – It's . . . . Gray.

30. stranger – foreigner

a) 1. Sorry, I can't show you the way; I'm a . . . . here myself. 2. There were a lot of Frenchmen and other . . . .s at our hotel.
b) 1. Your English is so good, you must be a . . . . ! 2. Our dog always barks at . . . .s. 3. Having been in prison for eight years, he came like a . . . . into his own house.

○ **31. to lead – to guide – to conduct**

a) 1. The orchestra was . . . . by Leonard Bernstein. 2. He is a . . . .ing member of the Labour Party. 3. Do you think that the boy can . . . . us up the mountain?
b) 1. The troops were . . . . by the general himself. 2. A new and more powerful class of . . . .ed missile ships will be equipped with new surface-to-air . . . .ed weapons. 3. Being a traveller for a big firm, he . . . .s a very irregular life. 4. Mr Kissinger has . . . . American foreign policy for years though he did not become Secretary of State until September 1973. 5. The Scout . . . . the blind man across the road. *(past tense)* 6. Every summer, London Transport runs its famous . . . .ed coach tours.

°**32. all – whole – entire – complete – total – quite**

a) 1. I've got a .... edition of Shakespeare's works. 2. She does not feel .... well. 3. I've been waiting for you .... the time. 4. The .... sum he lost by gambling amounts to £ 5,000. 5. You must tell me the .... truth about the matter. 6. Up to now my assistant has done everything to my .... satisfaction.

b) 1. It has been raining now for three .... days. 2. Rain or sunshine – it's .... the same to me. 3. .... darkness prevented the police from finding any footprints around the house. 4. These lamps are .... the thing I'd like to have for my sitting room. 5. The things stored in the loft of the old house were .... covered with dust. 6. The .... timber yard was destroyed by fire; it was ....ly surrounded by houses and blocks of flats. 7. His attempt to get a rise in salary was a .... failure. 8. You must do your homework now. Is that .... clear? 9. Your kite is smashing, John; did you make it .... on your own? 10. You must consider the plan as a ....; we can talk about the details later.

33. to go – to walk

a) 1. As we had missed the bus, we had to ..... 2. It's time for you to .... to bed now.

b) 1. The best way to get to the theatre from here is to .... on foot. 2. The baby cannot yet ..... 3. Shall we .... or drive to the cinema? – Let's ...., it's not far from here. 4. On Saturday we must .... shopping. 5. I sometimes .... to school, but usually I .... by bus.

°**34. mind – spirit – genius – ghost**

a) 1. The .... of liberty cannot be suppressed. 2. He looked as if he had seen a ..... 3. Shakespeare was the greatest .... in English literature. 4. So many men, so many ....s.

b) 1. Out of sight, out of ..... 2. Hamlet saw the .... of his father. 3. What he did offends against the .... of the law though not against the letter. 4. Your good .... made you come here in time. 5. She gave up the .... before her son arrived. 6. She could never make up her .....

35. occasion – opportunity – chance – facility

a) 1. Let's give him a .... to show his abilities. 2. At the first .... I'll tell him not to spend too much money on his hobbies. 3. On this .... he told me that he wanted to marry her. 4. Our school library is excellent and there are quite a lot of ....s for extra study.

b) 1. I'm glad to have this .... of speaking to you alone. 2. The prisoners had no .... of escape. 3. I met him on the .... of his sister's wedding. 4. Such ....s should not be missed.

°**36. company – society – party**

a) 1. It is better to be alone than in bad ..... 2. We'll have a .... next Saturday. 3. The Royal .... of London for the Advancement of Science was founded in 1660.

b) 1. The abolition of slavery is a characteristic of a civilized ..... 2. In 1670 the Hudson's Bay .... was formed to develop the fur trade with North America. 3. Waiter: "Sorry, sir, the restaurant's closed; there's a private ....."

°**37. healthy – sound – wholesome – sane**

a) 1. A .... mind in a .... body. 2. Sometimes one doesn't know if he's .... or mad. 3. Early to bed and early to rise makes a man ...., wealthy and wise. 4. You should eat good .... food, especially fruit and vegetables.

b) 1. You'll never get rid of your bronchitis here. What you need is a .... climate. 2. In spite of a lot of difficulties during the journey we arrived safe and ..... 3. You should take his advice; it might be very .... to you. 4. His way of living is very .....

38. happiness – fortune – luck

a) 1. Every man is the architect of his own . . . . . 2. I wish you good . . . . in the competition. 3. When she heard that her son had been rescued, she was overcome by an immense feeling of . . . . .

b) 1. . . . . favours the brave. 2. One of my friends had the . . . . to inherit a building site in downtown Manhattan. 3. He made his . . . . by selling it for a lot of money. 4. But though he is wealthy now, he has not found . . . . yet.

39. big – large – tall – great – grand – huge – vast

a) 1. There are . . . . car parks round the stadium. 2. Fred is a . . . . boy; he stands six feet. 3. It was a . . . . idea to spend the holidays on board a ship. 4. Nellie wants to be a doctor when she is . . . . . 5. There are . . . . fields of wheat in the prairies of central Saskatchewan. 6. Abraham Lincoln was one of the . . . .est presidents of the United States. 7. The new bank is a . . . . building.

b) 1. A man with a . . . . family needs a . . . . house. 2. That was a . . . . mistake. 3. We had a . . . . time at the party yesterday. 4. The Gobi Desert is a . . . . stretch of desert country entirely surrounded by . . . . mountains. 5. Elephants are . . . . animals; giraffes are . . . . . 6. Are you as . . . . as your brother? 7. Julius Caesar was a . . . . statesman. 8. The . . . . Duke of Luxembourg. 9. The yacht had a . . . . mast.

° **40. ground – reason – cause – motive**

a) 1. What was his . . . . for leaving his wife? 2. There are no . . . .s for calling him a cheat. 3. I have good . . . . to believe that he won't come. 4. The consumption of shellfish caught in the harbour of Naples is said to have been the . . . . of the cholera epidemic in Italy in 1973.

b) 1. I don't think you have any . . . . to say such a thing. 2. During the recent war in the Near East we all hoped that there were no . . . .s for intervention by one of the super powers. 3. Envy is his only . . . . for constantly attacking his brother. 4. She is always complaining without . . . . .

Situational Practice (21–40)

Just for Fun

1. The taxi started with a jerk and raced madly along through dense traffic.
Woman: "Please, be careful, this is the first time I've ever . . . . *(gefahren)* in a taxi."
Driver: "And this is the first time I've ever . . . . *(gefahren)* one."

2. Office boy: "A . . . . *(Dame)* to see you, sir."
Manager: "Is she pretty?"
Boy: "Yes – very."
Manager: "Show her in."
Manager (later): "You seem to have a strange idea of female beauty, boy."
Boy: "Well, sir, I thought she might be your . . . . *(Frau)*."
Manager: "She was."

3. Oliver, with a half-smoked cigarette in his mouth, entered a bus. When the conductor saw the cigarette, he said rather rudely, "No smoking here!" Oliver looked at his cigarette, which was out, and replied, "I'm not smoking." – "You've got a cigarette in your mouth, though." – "I've got my shoes on but I'm not . . . . *(gehen)*."

4. The .... *(Frau)* was trying to get her .... *(Mann)* to buy a new car, but he did not like the idea.
"Do you think that automobiles grow on trees?" he asked.
"Of course not, silly," replied his .... *(Frau)*. "Everyone knows they come from *plants*."

See a Pin and Pick it up

A .... *(Herr)* from Stockholm, who was on business in London, was once invited to a .... *(Gesellschaft)* in the house of the owner of a .... *(großen)* paper .... *(Fabrik)* on the .... *(Gelegenheit, Anlaß)* of a profitable business transaction. An excellent meal was served with good wines and all sorts of .... *(Fleisch)*, vegetables and salads. When they had .... *(fertig waren mit)* eating, the .... owner's .... *(Frau)* .... *(führte)* her .... *(Mannes)* guest into the garden, where her eyes fell upon a small pin lying in the middle of the garden path. "Oh," she said," in England there's an old saying: See a pin and pick it up and .... *(den ganzen)* that day you'll have good .... *(Glück)*."
After a pleasant afternoon the Swede said good-bye to his hosts and made up his .... *(entschloß sich)* to .... *(gehen)* back to his hotel; he was a .... *(gesunder)* man and the distance was not too .... *(groß)*. As the weather was fine, he sat down on a bench. Suddenly his eyes fell upon a small pin lying on the road near his bench. When he bent to pick it up, his glasses fell and broke on the pavement; he opened his mouth in surprise and lost his .... *(falschen)* teeth. Then he was nearly .... over *(überfahren)* by a lorry. .... *(ganz)* embarrassed, he arrived at a bus stop. On the bus he realized two things at the same time: the back of his coat was covered with wet .... *(Farbe)* and he had got into the .... *(falschen)* bus. He saw that it was a .... *(großer)* .... *(Fehler)* to think that English sayings were in any way applicable to .... *(Fremden)*.

3. Group Three: Numbers 41–60

○ **41. harbour – dock – port**

a) 1. There are about 80,000 .... workers employed by the National .... Labour Board. 2. Portsmouth is a naval .... . 3. After three days in a heavy sea, we were glad to be in the .... again.
b) 1. The .... of London is, with New York and Rotterdam, one of the three largest ....s in the world. Goods of every kind pass through the ....s. 2. Though the island was small, it had a good .... . 3. There are over three hundred ....s in Britain.

42. to hold – to keep

a) 1. In fine weather I always .... my window open. 2. Will you please .... my umbrella for a moment?
b) 1. An apple a day ....s the doctor away. 2. The box is so old that it will not .... together. 3. The meetings are .... once a month. 4. These curtains are meant to .... off the mosquitoes. 5. He ....s bees; he has got about 80 beehives. 6. The little girl was ....ing her father's hand. 7. .... off the grass! 8. Where do you .... your money? 9. These shoes will .... your feet warm. 10. (Telephonist:) .... the line, please. 11. When you make a speech, you must .... strictly to your subject. 12. When we approached him, he was ....ing a stick in his hand. 13. If I had not .... him back, he would have beaten you. 14. The room must be .... in order. 15. Let me take a photograph; .... still for a moment.

○ **43. heap – pile**

a) 1. There were ....s of dirt and rubbish in the streets. 2. I've got a big .... of letters on my desk; they must be answered within the next two weeks.
b) 1. The tulip bulbs were lying on the ground in ....s. 2. Dagobert Duck has got ....s of money. 3. The waiter stumbled over the threshold with a .... of plates in his hands.

44. sky – heaven

a) 1. Do you see the kite in the ....? 2. In the beginning God created .... and earth.
b) 1. We had to spend the night under the open ..... 2. No master ever dropped from the ....s. 3. She looked like an angel from ..... 4. When we left the house, the .... was overcast, and soon afterwards it began to rain.

45. to hear – to listen (to)

a) 1. When I walked through the park, I .... a bird sing. 2. I stopped and .... the bird's song for a while.
b) 1. Don't .... her; she's a silly goose. 2. How often do you .... from your brother in Calcutta? 3. When they .... the noise, they all .... *(past tense)*. 4. I can't .... what he's saying. 5. None are so deaf as those that will not ..... 6. I .... his speech, but did not .... anything I had not .... before.

○ **46. to hunt – to chase – to shoot**

a) 1. My brother is in Africa, ...ing lions. 2. The submarine was .... by several destroyers. 3. In England foxes are often .... on horseback.
b) 1. Lose an hour in the morning and you will be all day ....ing for it. 2. .... the dog out of the garden. 3. Mr Brown has gone out ....ing birds near the bog. 4. He has a terrible fear of dogs. He was once .... into a cemetery by a pack of wild dogs.

47. each – every – any – either

a) 1. These peaches cost two pence ..... 2. He is taller than .... of you two. 3. You are seriously ill; .... doctor can tell you that. 4. We go to church .... Sunday.
b) 1. Which pair of scissors do you want? – .... one will do. 2. The teacher asked .... of the boys in the class. 3. It's raining. Which of the three umbrellas may I take? – Oh, you may take .... of them. 4. .... of the twins is good at swimming. 5. He's a man who will do ....thing for money. 6. .... child must go to school. 7. .... of us has done his duty. 8. She came to see her mother .... other day.

○ **48. channel – canal**

a) 1. The Manchester Ship .... made Manchester one of England's leading ports. 2. It is improbable that the .... tunnel will be built soon.
b) 1. The Suez .... was reopened in 1975. 2. The Rhine and the Elbe are connected by a system of ....s. 3. St George's .... is between Wales and Ireland.

○ **49. cushion – pillow**

a) 1. When her mother came in, she jumped into her bed and hid the letter under the ..... 2. A fat dog was sleeping on the sofa with his head lying on a .....
b) 1. This chair is not very comfortable; can I have a ...., please? 2. We must ask the landlady to bring us new .... cases.

50. to cook – to boil – to make
a) 1. My wife knows how to . . . . . 2. Father is coming home; we must . . . . tea for him. 3. Be careful, the milk is going to . . . . over.
b) 1. He was . . . .ing with anger. 2. He is not married; he . . . .s all his meals himself. 3. I want some . . . .ing water to . . . . a cup of instant coffee.

○ **51. strength – force – power – vigour**
a) 1. We had to use . . . . to open the box. 2. In his speech he showed great . . . . . 3. It is beyond his . . . . to lend you such a lot of money. 4. The . . . . of an elephant is greater than that of a horse.
b) 1. His . . . . of mind helped him to overcome all difficulties. 2. The Ministry of . . . . used to have the duty of ensuring the effective development of fuel and . . . . supplies in Britain. 3. He pulled at the rope with great . . . .; he pulled at the rope with all his . . . . . 4. The child is in the . . . . of kidnappers. 5. The . . . . of the box resisted the . . . . of the blow.

52. ill – sick
a) 1. . . . . children must stay in bed. 2. When children are . . . ., they must stay in bed.
b) 1. You look . . . . . 2. Grandfather is lying . . . . in bed. 3. Have you ever been sea. . . .? 4. It makes me . . . . to think of the exam. 5. How long has she been . . . . now? 6. She went to the hospital to visit the . . . . .

○ **53. coast – shore – beach – bank**
a) 1. A rocky . . . . is dangerous. 2. Our house was built on the . . . . of a small river. 3. We were glad to be on . . . . again. 4. The children have been playing on the . . . . all day.
b) 1. Massachusetts is one of the original states along the Atlantic . . . . . 2. We had spent all the afternoon on the . . . . looking for shells and crabs when we suddenly saw a strange boat not far from the . . . . . 3. In America the Lighthouse Service is part of the . . . . Guard. 4. Cleveland lies on the . . . . of Lake Erie.

54. land – country
a) 1. Did you travel by air or by . . . .? 2. Nigeria is one of the most populous . . . .s in Africa.
b) 1. My uncle has got one house in London and another in the . . . . . 2. The government gave some . . . . to the poor. 3. On the 103rd day of their voyage the poor sailors saw . . . . again. 4. In Florence you'll find a lot of fellow . . . .men of yours.

55. empty – vacant
a) 1. He drank very fast; his glass was always . . . . . 2. There are some . . . . seats in this compartment.
b) 1. The throne has been . . . . since the old queen died. 2. I want some . . . . cigar boxes for my slides. 3. Do you think I might have got a stomach-ache just because my tummy is . . . .? 4. The hotel was all booked up; only one attic room under the roof was . . . . .

56. to borrow – to lend
a) 1. My uncle often . . . .s money from my father. 2. Can you . . . . me ten dollars?
b) 1. Is that your car? – No, I . . . . it. – Who . . . . it to you? 2. May I . . . . your ballpen? 3. Please return the books you . . . . from me. 4. A bank . . . .s money and charges interest. 5. I want to go to the . . . .ing library to . . . . some books.

57. to make – to do – (to take)
a) 1. How many photos did you . . . . ? 2. Can you . . . . a pancake? 3. Let me . . . . the washing-up tonight.
b) 1. The president . . . . only a short speech at the dinner *(past tense)*. 2. Don't forget to . . . . your homework. 3. . . . . it yourself. 4. After I've . . . . a lot of repairs on my car, it . . . .s 80 miles an hour again. 5. What are you . . . .ing there? I'm . . . .ing a box for my stamps. 6. Let's . . . . a fire and . . . . some tea. 7. Jane is . . . .ing her sums; she has . . . . a lot of mistakes already. 8. . . . . hay while the sun shines. 9. Let's . . . . a walk through the park. 10. Next week the boys will . . . . examinations; they will . . . . their best to pass. 11. . . . . up your mind and . . . . it quickly. 12. He has come to London to . . . . business. 13. 2 + 2 . . . . 4. 14. What is this box . . . . of? 15. Don't . . . . so much noise. 16. The first thing you must . . . . when you get up is to . . . . your bed and to . . . . the bedroom. 17. This is the way to . . . . it. 18. All that you . . . ., ... it with your might; things . . . . by halves are never . . . . right. 19. My grandmother had a maid to . . . . her housework. 20. to . . . . preparations, ... a test, ... a journey, ... friends, ... a discovery, ... a puzzle, ... one's duty, ... an exercise, ... use of, ... wrong, ... a fool of oneself, ... room for, ... peace.

° **58. machine – engine**
a) 1. Sorry we're late; we've had . . . . trouble on the motorway. 2. Has your mother got a washing . . . . ?
b) Drivers should not leave their . . . . running when they wait at a level crossing. 2. One . . . . can run several . . . .s. 3. Is it hand-made or . . . .-made? 4. The flying club owns a two- . . . .ed plane.

° **59. to rent – to hire**
a) 1. Is this your own house? – No, we . . . . it. 2. Can we . . . . bicycles here?
b) 1. The storm blew down some big trees in our garden; I'm afraid we've got to . . . . some men to remove them. 2. You can . . . . a safe at your bank for documents and other valuables.

° **60. fog – mist – haze**
a) 1. When the ship sailed on, the famous skyline of Manhattan became clearer in the early morning . . . . . 2. Whenever I climbed Snowdon, the summit was in thick . . . . . 3. In the evening a veil of . . . . formed over the lake.
b) 1. The great London . . . . of Dec. 1952 killed about 4,000 persons and brought the activities of the metropolis almost to a halt. 2. When she awoke after the operation, she saw everything through a . . . . 3. A . . . .horn is used for warning ships in . . . . .

Situational Practice (41–60)

Just for Fun

1. Doctor Greenbury, who was noted for his politeness, was awakened one night at 4 a.m. by his telephone. "This is Mrs Tupper speaking", said an angry woman's voice. "Doctor, your dog is barking and . . . .ing *(halten)* me awake." Doctor Greenbury thanked her and hung up.
The following morning at four, Mrs Tupper's telephone rang. "Madam", said the Doctor, "I haven't got a dog."

2. Some tourists came to a small village in Wales and saw that the four church clocks showed different times. They asked an old man: "What's the good of four church clocks, ... *(jede)*

showing different times?" The old man replied: "And what's the good of four clocks, ... *(jede)* showing the same time?"

3. Mother: "What are you reading, dear?"
Child: "I don't know, Mummy."
Mother: "But you were reading aloud."
Child: "Yes, but I wasn't ....ing *(zuhören)*."

4. Employer to applicant: "Sorry I can't .... *(anheuern, anstellen)* you; we don't need any help now."
Applicant: "Well, sir, I wouldn't be much help."

Mrs Bunbury's Voyage

"...." *(höre)*, said Mrs Maxwell to her friend Mrs Bunbury, a widow. "You should not always be sitting on your couch between two ....s *(Haufen)* of books from the ....ing library *(Leihbücherei)*, reading from morning to night .... *(jeden)* day. What you should be ....ing *(machen)* is ....ing *(machen)* a voyage to see something of the world." Mrs Bunbury put the book she was ....ing *(hielt)* in her hands on a .... *(Kissen)* and promised to consider the idea.
Mrs Bunbury .... *(hielt)* her promise. The following day she began to .... *(machen)* preparations for a voyage to Egypt. First of all she went to the bank in order to .... *(leihen)* some money. Two weeks later she was on her way to Southampton, a .... *(Hafen)* on the English .... *(Kanal)*. When the ship was leaving the .... *(Hafen)*, there was not a cloud in the .... *(Himmel)* and Mrs Bunbury really enjoyed the voyage, sitting in a deck chair. Soon, however, when they were sailing along the .... *(Küste)* of France, a heavy storm began to blow and the ship was violently shaken by huge waves. When the storm reached its full .... *(Kraft)*, the dining room was nearly .... *(leer)* even at dinner time, because all the passengers were in their cabins – sea.... *(seekrank)*. During these days Mrs Bunbury did not enjoy the voyage.
Some days later there was no wind at all, but the boat had to move slowly in a very thick .... *(Nebel)*. .... *(jeder)* knows how dangerous fog is at sea. When the ....s *(Maschinen)* were stopped and the terrible sound of ....horns *(Nebelhörner)* could be .... *(gehört)* from far and near, Mrs Bunbury, rather frightened, asked a sailor: "For ....'s sake *(um Himmels willen)*, how far are we from .... *(Land)*?" – "Half a mile", he answered. – "Where is the .... *(Land)*?" The old lady wanted to know. – "Straight down," replied the sailor. Now Mrs Bunbury wished she were in her home .... *(Land)* with her ....s *(Haufen)* of books.

4. Group Four: Numbers 61–80

○ **61. packet – parcel – package**
a) 1. I posted a small .... to you the other day. 2. The men were carrying heavy ....s out of the shop. 3. Among other things the little boy had a .... of sweets in his bag.
b) 1. Postal clerk: "With those ....s you must go to the .... post counter." 2. Give me that .... of letters, please. 3. Letters get to England quicker than ....s do. 4. Do you want the rice loose or in a ....?

62. to fit – to suit – to match
a) 1. Those brown shoes do not .... your black suit. 2. This coat doesn't .... me; it's too big. 3. It is difficult to find a time that ....s everybody.

b) 1. If the cap . . . .s, wear it. 2. His clothes are ill-. . . .ing. 3. The house did not . . . . the pianist because his piano was too big to . . . . in any of the rooms. 4. Does a green hat . . . . me? 5. Jack and Jane are a well-. . . .ed pair. 6. It does not . . . . her to wear her hair so long.

○ **63. pause – interval – break – rest**
a) 1. Is there an . . . . between the two parts of the concert? 2. He is tired, he needs a . . . . . 3. We worked five hours without a . . . . . 4. A comma denotes a short . . . .; a semicolon a longer one.
b) 1. Lunch. . . . is from 12.45 to 2 o'clock. 2. There was a . . . . before he answered my question. 3. You need a long . . . . after your hard work. 4. The performance will be continued after an . . . . of 25 minutes. 5. We have a . . . . of 5 to 20 minutes after each lesson. 6. We had several . . . .s on our way up the mountain.

64. place – seat – room
a) 1. What's the name of this . . . .? 2. That wardrobe takes up too much . . . . . 3. I couldn't find a good . . . . in the train.
b) 1. These boxes are rather big; there's only . . . . for six of them. 2. Your . . . . is to the right of the chairman. 3. It would be difficult to find a man to take the . . . . of the present principal. 4. When does the meeting take . . . .? 5. I haven't much . . . . to move here.

65. price – prize
a) 1. I bought the car at a very low . . . . . 2. My sister has won a . . . . in a snapshot competition.
b) 1. . . . .s have been going up for years now. 2. The horse won several . . . .s last year. 3. You mustn't do it at any . . . . .

66. politics – policy
a) 1. All that he knows about . . . . he read in the newspapers. 2. Lots of people do not approve of the government's . . . . on inflation.
b) 1. The general . . . . of the party is laid down at annual party conferences. 2. When he was 80, he withdrew from . . . . .

○ **67. revenge – to revenge – vengeance – to avenge**
a) 1. He took . . . . on the cruel murderer of his sister. 2. I shall . . . . the wrong that you have done me. 3. His thirst for . . . . was insatiable. 4. Hamlet . . . .ed the murder of his father.
b) 1. Was it divine . . . . that the murderer was run over by a bus? 2. The father . . . .ed the wrong that had been done to his daughter. 3. He waited for an opportunity to have his . . . . .

○ **68. to govern – to rule – to reign**
a) 1. Queen Victoria . . . .ed for more than 60 years. 2. The king . . . .ed his people with justice. 3. Who are the men that really . . . . in this country?
b) 1. The despot . . . .ed with a rod of iron. 2. In 1910 South Africa became a self-. . . .ing dominion. 3. While the emperor . . . .ed, he never really . . . .ed but left the government in the hands of his ministers. 4. It was George V who in 1917 decreed that the . . . .ing family would henceforth be known by the surname of Windsor. 5. The people no longer wanted a king to . . . . over them.

69. journey – voyage – travel(s) – tour – trip
a) 1. You're going to Edinburgh tonight? I wish you a pleasant . . . . . 2. During our holiday we are going to make a . . . . of Scotland. 3. She became seasick on her . . . . to Australia. 4. He gave a lecture on his . . . . in Africa. 5. During the weekend he will take a . . . . to the seaside.

b) 1. About three and a half centuries ago the .... across the Atlantic was filled with dangers and hardships. 2. During his .... he learned a lot about foreign peoples and countries. 3. Because of the devaluation of the dollar the .... to Europe has become more expensive for Americans. 4. On our .... to Vienna we stopped in Salzburg. 5. A coach .... is the perfect way to view everything in comfort.

○ **70. rest – remains – relic(s)**

a) 1. Intensive excavation brought forth interesting .... of Maya civilization. 2. For the .... of his life he lived in Rome. 3. The .... of several kings of old are buried in Winchester Cathedral.

b) 1. Most of the tourists went to the swimming pool, the .... went to a museum. 2. Capital punishment is a .... of barbarism. 3. Near the village there are the .... of an old castle. 4. I hope he will be able to pay the .... of his debt soon.

○ **71. right – correct – proper – real**

a) 1. Is Nana her .... name? 2. He's the .... man in the .... place. 3. Your intonation of this sentence is not quite ..... 4. Do you think that this is the .... dress for that occasion?

b) 1. That serves him ..... 2. He always displayed .... behaviour. 3. It's .... tea, not blackberry leaves *(1984)*. 4. Does anybody know the .... way to address a duke? 5. Is this the .... way to Hampstead Heath?

○ **72. quiet – calm – still – silent**

a) 1. Our neighbours' children are very ..... 2. The child could not sit .... during the long sermon. 3. In autumn the weather in the Alps is often .... and sunny. 4. You'd better be .... about what you've just heard here.

b) 1. If you want me to take the fly out of your eye, you must keep .... for a moment. 2. You seem very .... today; what's the matter with you? 3. Mrs Dixon was quite .... when she heard that her husband had had an accident. 4. We must try to find a hotel where we can have a .... room looking onto the garden. 5. In the word 'debt' the 'b' is a .... letter. 6. .... waters run deep. 7. We were looking forward to a .... evening when suddenly the telephone rang.

○ **73. thing – matter – affair – business (concern) – cause – point**

a) 1. He always talks a lot, but he never comes to the ..... 2. Don't forget your swimming ....s. 3. I have to talk to you about a .... of great importance. 4. His ....s have been in a sad state for years. 5. We had to make common .... with him. 6. It's your .... to know of such things.

b) 1. Don't take ....s too seriously; take them as a .... of course. 2. When it came to the ...., he refused his help. 3. We heard a lot of interesting ....s at the meeting. 4. I didn't want to interfere with his ....s; it was no .... of mine. 5. ....s seem to be getting worse and worse. 6. Sorry, I can't help you with your decision; it's entirely a .... of taste. 7. You must stick to the ..... 8. A holiday in the mountains will be just the .... for him. 9. You had no .... to take part in the meeting. 10. She's so silent; there seems to be something the .... with her. 11. Have you cleared away your ....s?

74. to say – to tell *(a 1. 2., b 3. 8. 9. 13.: past tense)*

a) 1. The doctor .... him not to smoke too much. 2. The doctor .... to him: "Don't smoke too much."

b) 1. How can you .... which is the right one? 2. "Have you anything else to ....?" asked the judge. 3. Mr Gray .... he would like to stay at our school for another year. 4. When did he .... you that? 5. Let's go home together; shall we .... at one o'clock? 6. What did he .... when he heard the news? 7. I can't .... you how happy we were. 8. Who .... so? 9. Who .... you so? 10. You never can .... what he'll do next. 11. I've something to .... to you. 12. Do you always .... the truth? 13. The policeman .... her not to park her car there. 14. Have you .... your father what I .... to you? 15. When did you .... he would return?

75. shade – shadow

a) 1. Let's sit in the ..... 2. In the evening the .... of the house grew longer and longer.
b) 1. These flowers will only grow in the ..... 2. The dog tried to chase his own ..... 3. It's nice to lie in the .... of these large trees. 4. Coming events cast their ....s before them.

76. to seem – to appear – to shine *(a 1., b 2. 3. 4. 6.: past tense)*

a) 1. He suddenly .... in front of us. 2. The sun was ....ing. 3. It ....s to me that something is wrong.
b) 1. It ....s impossible. 2. It .... afterwards that he had made a mistake. 3. After the rain the sun .... again in the sky. 4. A light .... out into the darkness. 5. He does not .... to have any money. 6. Her jewels .... in the lamp light. 7. She ....s to be quite happy.

○ **77. to strike – to hit – to beat** *(a 1. 2., b 3. 4.: past tense)*

a) 1. Tom.... the other boy on the nose with his clenched fist. 2. They .... him black and blue. 3. That ....s the nail on the head.
b) 1. His heart stopped ....ing. 2. Did Sam .... Jack at tennis? 3. She .... me with her book. 4. He .... at me, but he didn't .... me. 5. She accused her husband of ....ing her. 6. We saw the farmer ....ing the dog with a stick. 7. It has just .... five. 8. The rain was ....ing against the window.

○ **78. to shut – to close – to lock – to conclude**

a) 1. What do you .... from his behaviour? 2. The shops .... daily at six o'clock. 3. .... your books, please. 4. The gate was ....ed and we had no key.
b) 1. The office is ....ed on Saturdays. 2. I got home late last night and found myself ....ed out. 3. As you didn't say a word, we ....ed that you agreed to our proposal. 4. .... your eyes for a moment. 5. She has ....ed her eyes for ever. 6. I must now .... my letter. 7. She ....ed up her jewels in a safe.

79. beautiful – handsome – pretty – fine – fair – nice

a) 1. There are a lot of .... girls in our town. 2. The barometer stands at ..... 3. That's not .... of you. 4. The weather was .... all the time we were in Bournemouth. 5. He's a tall and .... man. 6. Her mother is still a .... woman.
b) 1. They worked hard and made quite a .... profit. 2. It's .... and warm by the fire. 3. It's .... warm, isn't it? 4. These flowers are truly ..... 5. Ladies are often referred to as the .... sex.

80. debt – fault – guilt

a) 1. I hope he can pay his ....s now. 2. Has his .... been proved now or is it still in doubt? 3. Whose .... is it?
b) 1. After all the witnesses had been heard, the .... of the accused was evident. 2. It was my .... that he lost so much money. 3. I remain in your .... for this amount.

Situational Practice (61–80)

Just for Fun

1. Postal clerk: "Yes, madam, you have enough stamps on this .... *(Paket)*. In fact you have three cents too much on it."
Woman: "Oh, how dreadful! Does that mean it might go too far?"

2. "I've come from the Employment Exchange, madam," said the girl. "They .... *(sagten)* me you wanted a servant maid."
"But I do all the work myself," replied the lady of the house.
"Then the place will just .... *(passen)* me, madam."

3. My husband is so tender-hearted that he won't .... *(schlagen)* the children. —
My husband is so tender-hearted that he won't even help to .... *(schlagen, klopfen)* the carpets.

4. Jane: "My boyfriend has been ....ing *(sagen)* everyone that he is going to marry the most .... *(schönste)* girl in the whole world."
Joan: "What a shame! And after all the time you two have been going together."

The Opportunity

One afternoon a gentleman entered the post office to post a .... *(Paket)* and to buy some stamps. The clerk tore the stamps from the sheet and looking up, ... *(sagte)*, "Haven't I the honour of speaking to Mr Simpson?"
"That's .... *(richtig)*", ... *(sagte)* the gentleman.
"How are you, Mr Simpson and your family? Well, I hope the weather will remain .... *(schön)*. It was 28 degrees in the .... *(Schatten)* at noon."
Mr Simpson did not .... *(sagen)* a word and listened ....ly *(ruhig)*.
"What do you think of the government's .... *(Preispolitik)?* Whose .... *(Schuld)* is it that .... *(Preise)* have shot up again? By the way, your green hat .... *(paßt zu)* your coat."
Mr Simpson grew impatient, "Would it be possible – ?"
The clerk went on without a .... *(Pause)*. "Do you know that Mr Lee is deep in .... *(Schulden)?* He wanted to make a .... *(Reise)* of Europe, but now I'm afraid he – "
Mr Simpson became scarlet with anger and shouted: "You'd better mind your own .... *(Sache)*. Can I have my stamps now? The post office will .... *(schließen)* in a few minutes."
The clerk smiled. No sign of offence .... *(erschien)* on his face. "Of course exactly as Mr Simpson wishes. Perhaps you need some more stamps for abroad? Or some postal orders or telegram forms?"
Mr Simpson was near to ....ing *(schlagen)* the clerk in the face. Then he disappeared without bothering to reply.
The clerk's colleagues, who had heard the conversation, asked him: "What's the meaning of that?"
The clerk murmured: "...." *(Rache)*.
"...." *(Rache)?* Why's that?"
"That man is my hairdresser. He never allows me to get out of my .... *(Platz)* before he has .... *(gesagt)* me a lot of foolish ....s *(Sachen)* and offered me his whole range of soaps and shampoos. I've always been longing for this opportunity to .... *(rächen)* myself.

5. Group Five: Numbers 81–100

81.1 heavy – difficult – hard – serious (grave)

a) 1. That question is . . . . to answer. 2. The mistake is not very . . . . . 3. The box is too . . . . for us to carry. 4. He was used to working . . . . .

b) 1. Lead is a . . . . metal. 2. Woodcutting is . . . . , but not . . . . work. 3. The pain was . . . . to bear. 4. English is among the easiest languages to speak badly, but the most . . . . to use well. 5. His behaviour will have . . . . consequences. 6. Who is . . . . weight champion at the moment? 7. He tried . . . . to succeed.

81.2 light – easy – slight

a) 1. This box is . . . .er than that one. 2. There's only a very . . . . difference between the two. 3. This story is . . . . to understand.

b) 1. It was raining . . . .ly when we left the house. 2. He has been . . . .ly injured. 3. It's . . . . for you to say that. 4. This boxer is a(n) . . . .weight. 5. That's a(n) . . . . question. 6. I want a pair of . . . . shoes for the summer. 7. Take it . . . . 8. It was only a(n) . . . . error.

° **82. to swim – to float**

a) 1. Next year some Americans will try to . . . . the Channel. 2. Look, there's a raft . . . .ing on the river.

b) 1. Tea chests and tea leaves were . . . .ing in Boston harbour. 2. It's not easy to . . . . against the stream. 3. Our dog . . . . across the river last night. 4. Does rubber sink or . . . . ?

83. to see – to look – to gaze (to stare) – to glance

a) 1. Are you still . . . .ing for a job? 2. The little boy was . . . .ing at the toys in the shop window. 3. He . . . .ed quickly over the page. 4. We can't . . . . in the dark.

b) 1. My father will be happy to . . . . you. 2. I . . . . up from my newspaper, and . . . . my friend Norman, whom I had not . . . . for years, sitting opposite me. 3. He . . . .s like a fool. 4. The officer . . . .ed at my passport without much care and told me to drive on. 5. What can you . . . . when you . . . . out of the window? 6. The child . . . .ed fixedly at the funny hat of the lady opposite her. 7. What are you . . . .ing at? 8. Can you . . . . the man on the roof? 9. She . . . .s very tired.

° **84. rare – scarce – seldom (rarely)**

a) 1. Those trees are very . . . . in this country. 2. Oil is getting . . . . now. 3. Barking dogs . . . . bite.

b) 1. Food was . . . . during the war. 2. He . . . . writes to his parents. 3. It was a . . . . opportunity to see him alone.

85. sure – certain – safe – secure

a) 1. You won't be . . . . from discovery here for long. 2. I'm . . . . I left the keys in the cupboard. 3. It is quite . . . . that the ship has already left the harbour. 4. He was very ill, but the doctor says he's . . . . now.

b) 1. Your jewels are in a . . . . place. 2. One thing is . . . . , the money is lost. 3. Her name is Joan or Jane Williams; I'm not . . . . about her Christian name. 4. He has a . . . . income. 5. The best way to be . . . . is never to feel too . . . . . 6. On this island you are . . . . from your pursuers. 7. It is . . . . to rain. 8. A lot of people still think that travelling by car is . . . .er than travelling by air. 9. There were burglars in our neighbourhood last night. Are you . . . . that the doors and windows are . . . . ? 10. Under . . . . conditions I'm willing to accept your offer.

○ **86. to save – to spare**
a) 1. My friends . . . .ed neither time nor money in order to help me. 2. Did he go by car only in order to . . . . time?
b) 1. A penny . . . .ed is a penny earned. 2. During these weeks before Christmas I cannot . . . . a minute. 3. She's . . . .ing for a new bicycle. 4. . . . . the rod and spoil the child.

87. play – game – match
a) 1. I can't call that fair . . . . . 2. A baseball . . . . usually lasts between two and three hours. 3. Hockey is a . . . . that is played by men as well as by women.
b) 1. Cricket is England's national summer . . . . . Thousands of people turn out to see a . . . . between two English county teams. 2. Have you seen any of Arthur Miller's . . . .s? 3. Let's play . . . .s tonight. 4. "All work and no . . . . makes Jack a dull boy," Tom said to David as he was doing his Maths problem. "So let's go and see the baseball . . . ." – "All right," David replied, "but I don't know the . . . . ."

○ **88. to jump – to spring – to leap – to bound (to bounce)** *(a 1. 2., b 2. 3. 4.: past tense)*
a) 1. The dog . . . . at the thief's throat. 2. My heart . . . . with joy at this news. 3. This is a good ball; it . . . .s very high. 4. Can you . . . . over the ditch?
b) 1. Snack bars have . . . . up like mushrooms. 2. The little monkey . . . . about its cage like a ball. 3. He . . . . down the stairs and broke a leg. 4. When he entered, they . . . . up from their seats and welcomed him.

○ **89. street – road**
a) 1. The children were playing in the . . . . . 2. This . . . . leads to town.
b) The . . . .s of old towns are usually narrow. 2. Did you come by . . . . or by rail? 3. They are making a new . . . . here. 4. The man in the . . . . .

○ **90. piece – bit – fragment – lump – play**
a) 1. 'The Caretaker' is Pinter's most successful . . . . . 2. The old lady fed the dog with . . . .s of sugar. 3. Give me a . . . . of your bun. 4. A five-cent . . . . is called a nickel. 5. It was a difficult task, to put the . . . .s of the broken vase together.
b) 1. The plate is broken to . . . .s. 2. As there was something wrong with our radio, we could only hear . . . .s of the concert. 3. He has saved me a nice . . . . of money. 4. I have a . . . . of good news for you. 5. All the chief characters die at the end of the . . . . . 6. A . . . . of clay fell from the lorry just in front of my feet.

○ **91. action – act – deed**
a) 1. Was it an . . . . of self-defence? 2. A Boy Scout is expected to do a good . . . . every day. 3. He is insane and not responsible for his. . . .s.
b) 1. The . . . . of Wilder's 'Our Town' is very simple, but it is not what the play is about. 2. He was punished for his cruel . . . . . 3. The burglar was caught in the very . . . . of breaking into the house. 4. The play has five . . . .s. 5. You should judge a man by his . . . .s, not by his words.

92. to carry – to bear – to wear – to support
a) 1. The pain seemed too great to . . . . . 2. She was . . . .ing a new hat. 3. I cannot . . . . the box; it's too heavy. 4. The hall was so large that pillars were needed to . . . . the ceiling.
b) 1. What date does the letter . . . .? 2. American policemen . . . . colts and bullets in their belts. 3. She . . . .s her hair short. 4. Atlas . . . .s the sky on his shoulders. 5. The ice was too thin to . . . . the weight of such a lot of people. 6. American boys and girls do not . . . . school uniforms. 7. He was . . . .ing a bundle in his arms. 8. When he left the house in the morning,

he was ....ing an overcoat. When he came home for lunch, he was ....ing the coat on his arm.

○ **93. to entertain – to amuse – to enjoy – to rejoice – to delight (to be delighted)**

a) 1. My mother ....s in telling stories about my childhood. 2. I hope you'll .... yourself during your holidays. 3. How shall we .... our guests? 4. 'Three men in a boat' is a very ....ing book. 5. No one ....ed at her success more than her mother.

b) 1. She can .... herself for hours just watching the people go by. 2. Did you .... the play last night? 3. It is often difficult to .... small children at a birthday party. 4. What is ....ing you so? 5. I ....ed my last visit to London very much. 6. On my last visit to London I ....ed myself very much. 7. We all .... at your good fortune. 8. He is ....ed at getting a rise in pay. 9. "I hope you ....ed yourself at the party." – "Oh, yes, there was nothing else to .... ." 10. The children were much ....ed on Christmas morning. 11. I .... swimming and lying in the sun. 12. I .... to hear that you are well again.

94. to distinguish – to differ / distinction – difference

a) 1. One should not make ....s between persons on account of their race, colour or religion. 2. That book ....s from all the others in several respects. 3. I don't see any .... between the two. 4. He cannot .... Scotch whisky from Bourbon.

b) 1. The American system of government ....s considerably from the British. 2. She made a .... where there was no ..... 3. In this question I .... from you. 4. The .... in price is enormous. 5. The pictures were so much alike that we could not .... one from the other.

○ **95. to pursue – to persecute – to prosecute**

a) 1. The troops ...ed the enemy until midnight. 2. He was ....ed for stealing. 3. These people were ....ed for their faith.

b) 1. As their horses were tired, they could not .... the robbers any longer. 2. They will .... him for fraud. 3. Bad luck ....ed him everywhere. 4. During World War II the Jews were most cruelly ....ed. 5. Is it worth while ....ing the matter?

96. to choose – to select – to elect – to vote

a) 1. From a number of books he .... Orwell's 'Animal Farm'. 2. Next year a new Parliament will be ..... 3. You may .... what you like. 4. Every person of 18 years of age is entitled to .... in an election.

b) 1. Abraham Lincoln was .... President in 1860. 2. We .... him for our speaker *(past tense)*. 3. The majority of people in this area .... Labour. 4. Harold, Earl of Wessex, was .... King by the Saxons.

97. to become – to get – to grow – to turn *(a 4., b 1. 3.: past tense)*

a) 1. Our doctor is ....ing very old now. 2. He has .... a rich man by selling the greater part of his farm to a building firm. 3. I've been working from morning to night; I'm ....ing tired now. 4. At that news she .... pale.

b) 1. Elizabeth II .... Queen of England in 1952. 2. It's ....ing late, aren't you ....ing hungry? 3. The sky suddenly .... black, the wind .... stronger, and we .... wet. 4. It is autumn now and the days are ....ing shorter and shorter. 5. What will .... of his wife if he falls ill?

○ **98. sign – signal – token – mark**

a) 1. The horse has a white .... between its eyes. 2. There was no .... that the tools had ever been used. 3. The old man gave her a present as a .... of his gratitude. 4. At a given .... the soldiers began to attack the village.

b) 1. A red flag was placed on the beach as a .... of danger. 2. The murder of the general was the .... for revolt. 3. The years had left their ....s on his face. 4. Is it a good ....? 5. Generosity is the .... of a civilized man. 6. He gave us a .... to approach. 7. Take this gift as a .... of our regard for your services.

99. to show – to point

a) 1. The teacher ....ed at the girl in the picture. 2. The teacher ....ed the children some pictures.

b) 1. Please .... me what you have in that box. 2. .... out the boy who did it. 3. Can you .... me how to do it? 4. The hands of the clock ....ed to half past seven. 5. It is rude to .... at people.

○ **100. to draw – to pull – to drag** *(a 1.3., b 2.3.: past tense)*

a) 1. The thieves .... the heavy box across the yard. 2. In 1825 the first public passenger train was .... by Stephenson's locomotive 'Active'. 3. When he saw the boy in the river, he .... off his clothes and jumped into the water.

b) 1. The tea must .... for a few minutes. 2. He .... me by the sleeve. 3. The officer .... his sword. 4. I had a tooth .... out yesterday. 5. It is part of the election of Mr Speaker that two MPs physically .... him to the Speaker's Chair while he himself is putting up a show of resistance. 6. Can't you .... a straight line without a ruler?

Situational Practice (81–100)

Just for Fun

1. Most people can't understand why scientists are wasting their time trying to find intelligent beings on other planets when it is so .... *(schwer)* to find any of them here on earth.

2. The electrician was puzzled. "Hey", he called to his assistant, "put your hand on one of those wires." The assistant did as he was told. "Do you feel anything?" asked the electrician. "No, nothing", answered the assistant. "Good," said the electrician, "I wasn't .... *(sicher)* which was which. Don't touch the other end or you'll drop dead."

3. Teacher: "I should like you all to take more pride in your personal appearance. Now John, how many shirts do you .... *(tragen)* a week?"
John: "Please, teacher, do you mean how many weeks do I .... *(tragen)* a shirt?"

4. Sandra came home and announced with pride that she had been .... *(gewählt)* "the prettiest girl in the class". Her excitement was even greater the following day when she was .... *(gewählt)* "the most popular girl."
After another week and another election she was more subdued. When her parents pressed her for the reason, she finally admitted: "Today I was .... *(gewählt)* the most stuck-up girl in the class."

The Camel-Hair Coat

Mike had a brother. Mike's brother was a poor devil. .... *(selten)* had he more than a pound in his pocket, never had he been able to .... *(sparen)* any money. You could be .... *(sicher)* that he had a lot of .... *(Schulden)*. Mike, of course, helped his brother whenever he could though it was not .... *(leicht)* for him. He worked .... *(schwer)*, but it was .... *(schwer)* for him to .... *(ersparen, erübrigen)* the £ 40 he gave his brother every month.
One day Mike .... *(sah)* his brother from behind in the .... *(Straße)* some distance away. He could not help ....ing *(ansehen, anstarren)* at him in surprise, for his brother was ....ing

(trug) a very expensive camel-hair coat. Mike was speechless. What a .... *(Unterschied)* between his brother's elegant coat and his shabby, old one!

Mike followed his brother, who seemed to be in a great hurry, for he .... *(sah, blickte)* neither right nor left, but ran straight on. Mike tried to .... *(verfolgen)* him, he called and shouted. At last he reached him and, tapping him on the shoulder from behind, he said, "Wait a moment, Brother". ....ing *(zeigen)* at the coat, he added, "Where did you get that coat from?"

The other stopped and .... *(blickte, sah)* around with horror in his eyes. Mike .... *(wurde)* pale, it was not his brother. But before Mike could say a word, the stranger .... *(zog)* off the coat, handed it to Mike and said: "Well, if it's your coat, I hope you'll excuse me. I'm sorry, I'm in a hurry." And ....ing *(sehen, blicken)* at his watch, he disappeared into the crowd.

C. Cognate, Frequently Confused Words*)

77

1. Nouns

Put in the correct words.

○ **1. admission – admittance**
1. After his .... of the theft, he was sentenced to six months' imprisonment. 2. No .... except on business. 3. The .... of students to universities has become a difficult problem in Germany. 4. I don't know what the price of .... is. 5. We wanted to go for a walk in a private park, but we were refused .....

○ **2. affection – affectation**
1. The .... he expressed his silly ideas with was indeed ridiculous. 2. His wife is not the only object of his ..... 3. After he returned from a long journey, he was no longer sure of her .....

○ **3. appearance – apparition**
1. He has the .... of a wealthy man. 2. The .... had vanished from sight, but the woman was still staring at the window, trembling with fear. 3. The .... of the newspaper article called forth a wave of protest.

○ **4. application – appliance**
1. His .... for the job was rejected. 2. The fire-fighting ....s of the village were in a deplorable state. 3. The .... of new and very expensive remedies was useless; the patient died a few days later.

○ **5. armour – armament**
1. After World War II there were strong objections to German re-..... 2. Several old suits of .... are to be seen in the museum. 3. These destroyers have fully automatic ....s. 4. The steel .... protection of battleships varied in thickness, the heaviest being up to 19in.

---

*) About one half of the groups of words in this chapter are marked with a ○. This division is meant as a rough guide to their degree of difficulty or usefulness. It is recommended that students should begin with the unmarked numbers and resume the numbers with ○ later as more advanced learners.

6. bath – bathe

1. You can have hot and cold ....s there. 2. She wanted to have a .... in the sea, but she had forgotten her ....ing costume. 3. Where's Daddy? – He's still in the ....room.

7. bunch – bundle

1. The old man was carrying a .... of sticks on his back. 2. Bananas grow in ....s on trees in tropical countries. 3. The guest brought his hostess a .... of beautiful red roses.

8. cloth – clothing, clothes

1. We had to sleep in our .... as it was very cold in the hut. 2. The woman cleaned the floor with a ..... 3. The girl went to the party in her best ..... 4. Are you sure that you need two new table....? 5. Several articles of .... were found on the beach.

9. costume – custom

1. Most countries in the world have different ..... 2. My friend's father is a ....s officer. 3. We took a lot of pictures of the natives in their colourful national .....

○ **10. council – counsel**

1. The .... for the defence cross-examined the witness for more than an hour. 2. There will be another meeting of the .... next week. 3. The students often held .... with their teachers.

11. delivery – deliverance

1. In this village .... of parcels is only once a week. 2. The inhabitants of the besieged town waited anxiously for the moment of ..... 3. These goods are payable on .... .

○ **12. destiny – destination**

1. The ship did not reach her ..... 2. No man can fight against his ..... 3. We went on a journey in July; our .... was the Isle of Skye.

○ **13. disposal – disposition**

1. He employed all means at his ...., but without success. 2. We all like him because of his cheerful ..... 3. The .... of the old books and papers took us several days; we burnt most of them. 4. He had no .... to go to school again after having been ill for weeks.

14. emergence – emergency

1. The guard went along the length of the train asking who had pulled the .... brake. 2. We were prepared for every ..... 3. The .... of unforeseen problems complicated the matter.

15. experience – experiment

1. I had an unusual .... the other night. 2. The teacher did some .... with chlorine. 3. We all learn from .....

○ **16. expanse – expansion**

1. The government seeks to control the .... of industry in some areas and to encourage it in others. 2. A great .... of desert cuts off Arab North Africa from the rest of Africa. 3. The .... of our foreign trade will probably slow down.

○ **17. extent – extension**

1. The .... of the school building programme is a necessity. 2. The workers demanded an .... of their rights. 3. To what .... do you want to support him?

18. fraction – fracture
1. Can you do . . . . s? 2. You'd better have your arm X-rayed; it might be a . . . . . 3. It happened in a . . . . of a second.

○ **19. grief – grievance**
1. Question time gives an opportunity for calling the attention of the House of Commons to . . . . s and complaints of every kind. 2. His attempt to take over the bankrupt firm brought him to . . . . . 3. She is filled with . . . . .

20. lighting – lightning
1. The principal domestic uses of electricity are for . . . . , cooking and heating. 2. Have you got a . . . . conductor on your house? 3. The cat disappeared like . . . . .

21. liking – likeness
1. The tea is not to my . . . . . 2. The boy is the exact . . . . of his father. 3. There is a family . . . . in all of them.

○ **22. neglect – negligence**
1. The accident was due to . . . . . 2. The whole house was in a state of . . . . . 3. The child died throught the . . . . of its parents.

23. object – subject
1. The range of his knowledge of the . . . . seems to be unlimited. 2. The only . . . . of my visit is to warn you. 3. What was the . . . . you were talking about?

○ **24. observation – observance**
1. The . . . . of this regulation is essential. 2. The Jews said they would insist on strict . . . . of the Sabbath. 3. The experiment needed careful . . . . .

○ **25. pennies – pence**
1. Nowadays you can't use single . . . . in the phone boxes any longer. 2. The book costs 80 . . . . . 3. The old shilling was replaced by the new 5 . . . . piece.

○ **26. permission – permit**
1. He refused his daughter . . . . to use his car. 2. You need a . . . . to use this road. 3. She has my . . . . to stay here.

27. plain – plane
1. The . . . . extends for hundreds of miles. 2. Let's take the next . . . . to Chicago. 3. She is on the same low intellectual . . . . as her husband.

○ **28. precedent – precedence**
1. I can't allow you to cross my land because you might take it as a . . . . . 2. The titles of the members of the nobility are, in order of . . . . : Duke, Marquess, Earl, Viscount, Baron. 3. This question takes . . . . over all others.

○ **29. pretence – pretension**
1. The boy is constantly absent from school on the slightest . . . . . 2. As we had very little money, we entered a restaurant of no great . . . . s. 3. He came back under the . . . . of having forgotten something.

30. process – procedure
1. The first days of the conference were spent in arguing about questions of . . . . . 2. These measures are in full accordance with the rules of . . . . . 3. Our manufacturing . . . . is cheaper than theirs.

○ **31. produce – product**
1. The farmer could not make a living out of selling the . . . . of his fields. 2. Among the . . . . of the factory were cycles and agricultural machinery. 3. The old woman lived partly on the . . . . of her garden.

32. reception – receipt
1. The hotel has several . . . . rooms. 2. Who has signed the . . . . ? 3. The goods are payable on . . . . . 4. The ambassador held a . . . . last Friday.

33. secrecy – secret
1. This must remain a . . . . between us. 2. The strictest . . . . must be observed. 3. Can you keep a . . . . ?

34. stripe – strip
1. He prefers ties with red and blue . . . .s. 2. The detective found a blood-stained . . . . of cloth in the car. 3. Is he a sergeant or a corporal? He's got three . . . . on his uniform.

35. suspension – suspense
1. Our . . . . grew as the teacher opened the envelope with the examination papers. 2. The . . . . of payments had serious consequences for the firm. 3. We were kept in . . . . for weeks. 4. There was an outcry against the . . . . of the famous footballer.

○ **36. unity – union**
1. The . . . . of Soviet Socialist Republics is abbreviated to USSR. 2. It is doubtful if German . . . . will ever be restored. 3. The centre of the trade . . . . movement is the TUC (Trades U . . . . Congress).

○ **37. vacation – vacancy**
1. There are some . . . . for clerks in our firm. 2. My uncle is a university professor; during the long . . . . he'll come and see us.

2. Adjectives

78

Put in the correct words.

1. alone – lonely
1. He . . . . can do it. 2. We pitched our tent in a . . . . place in the Scottish Highlands. 3. The old woman cannot be left . . . . for more than a week.

○ **2. alternate – alternative**
1. The two schools use the swimming bath on . . . . days. 2. They watched at her bedside . . . .ly. 3. The tour may be made by road or . . . .ly by rail.

○ **3. beneficent – beneficial**
1. The cure had a most . . . . effect. 2. Being a wealthy man, he could easily be . . . . . 3. Frequent exercise will be . . . . to all of you.

4. careless – carefree

1. His father's wealth allowed him to live a .... existence. 2. I'm sorry to say that he did his work ....ly. 3. She is very .... with her money.

° **5. ceremonial – ceremonious**

1. This room is used only on .... occasions. 2. We were received with much .... politeness. 3. Why is he so ....? There's no need for ceremony among friends.

6. childish – childlike

1. Her obstinacy is quite ..... 2. There is no point in arguing with him; his opinions are rather ..... 3. The girl asked me with .... frankness if I liked her new dress.

° **7. comprehensive – comprehensible**

1. She gave me a .... list of all the things that had to be done. 2. This book is .... only to engineers. 3. As a commercial traveller who is on the road for about 50,000 miles a year he should take out .... insurance on his car.

° **8. confident – confidential**

1. Don't become too .... with him; you've known him for a short time only. 2. The soldiers were .... of victory. 3. The doctor is .... that this medicine will help you.

9. self-confident – self-conscious

1. She was too .... and shy to give him a piece of her mind in front of such a large audience. 2. He is a very .... young man who believes in his abilities.

10. conscious – conscientious

1. He has paid his debts ....ly. 2. Suddenly she was .... that someone else had entered the room. 3. She died three days after the accident; she was .... to the last.

° **11. contemptuous – contemptible**

1. That was a .... trick. 2. Instead of an answer he gave a .... smile. 3. He spoke ....ly of his brother.

° **12. content(ed) – to contend**

1. She is never .... with what she has got. 2. The explorers had to .... with terrible snowstorms. 3. He accepted the offer with a .... look.

° **13. continuous – continual**

1. We've had .... gales for three days now. 2. Performances in this cinema are .... from 11.15 a.m. to 10.30 p.m. 3. The .... noise of hammering disturbed us very much.

° **14. credible – credulous**

1. His excuse did not seem very ..... 2. The .... girl really believed the man when he promised to take her home. 3. There was no .... witness to prove what the accused had said.

° **15. defective – deficient**

1. The majority of cars examined by the police were ..... 2. Medical care and accomodation were .... in that hospital. 3. My camera is .....

16. definite – definitive
1. With the peace treaty the war was ....ly at an end. 2. This is my .... proposal; I'm not ready to modify it in any way. 3. It is a .... offer; the terms are unmistakable.

17. delightful – delicious
1. We spent a .... evening in his house. 2. The fruit we had was really ..... 3. This is the most .... book I've ever read.

18. desert – deserted
1. Only a dog was to be seen in the .... streets. 2. There are vast .... areas in North Africa. 3. The farm had been .... before the revengeful Sioux arrived.

°**19. desperate – despairing**
1. Seeing that the police had left him no chance to escape, the .... criminal took out his gun. 2. He made .... efforts to get out of his difficulties. 3. The deserter turned round to his wife and children with a last .... look before the soldiers pushed him into the car.

°**20. devoted – devout**
1. She is a .... old lady; she goes to church every morning. 2. The president could rely on a majority of .... supporters.

°**21. distinct – distinctive**
1. This problem is quite .... from the other. 2. When we entered the house there was a .... smell of gas. 3. Massive towers and walls and round arches are .... features of the Norman style.

°**22. effective (effectual) – efficient**
1. Miss Snell is an .... teacher. 2. Our co-operation was very ..... 3. Do you think that beating will be an .... punishment of the boy?

°**23. elementary – elemental**
1. I have only an .... knowledge of Italian. 2. The .... forces of the waves destroyed a part of the island. 3. .... education in England begins at the age of five.

°**24. enduring – endurable**
1. The pain was ..... 2. Let's hope that the result of the conference will be an .... peace. 3. Did you find the climate .... in Lagos?

°**25. envious – enviable**
1. Her husband is so nice; she is an .... woman. 2. She has always been .... of her sister. 3. He has got an .... position in a big firm.

°**26. exhausting – exhaustive**
1. He dealt with the subject ....ly. 2. Such a tour by coach is very .....

27. favourable – favourite
1. I can't say that cricket is my .... game. 2. We'll accept the offer if the conditions are ..... 3. Is History your .... subject?

28. German – Germanic
English, ... and Dutch are West .... languages.

29. gold – golden
1. These .... coins are valuable. 2. My parents had their .... wedding last year. 3. The time of Queen Elizabeth was the .... age of English drama.

30. honest – honourable – honorary
1. To be secretary of the club is an .... office. 2. He is .... in business. 3. His behaviour in this case was most ..... 4. ....ly, that's all I can give you.

○ **31. human – humane**
1. The new president promised a more .... treatment of the prisoners. 2. It is only .... to forget something sometimes.

32. humorous – good-humoured
1. Mark Twain is a .... writer. 2. The old man is always .....

33. illegal – illegitimate
1. In 1641 Parliament made up a list of all the .... acts of the king. 2. The prince was of .... descent.

○ **34. imaginable – imaginary – imaginative**
1. Shakespeare was a most .... dramatist. 2. That was the best solution ..... 3. Her illness seems to be only .....

○ **35. impressive – impressionable (impressible)**
1. Young people are more .... than older ones. 2. The investiture of Prince Charles as Prince of Wales was an .... ceremony. 3. His speech was not very .....

36. industrial – industrious
1. He is .... and efficient. 2. England became an .... country in the nineteenth century. 3. Bees are .... insects.

○ **37. ingenious – ingenuous**
1. An .... invention enabled him to produce such machines cheaper than his competitors. 2. She was so .... that she believed everything the salesman told her. 3. There can be no doubt of his .... character.

38. intelligent – intelligible – intellectual
1. He is a man of great .... abilities. 2. The little boy seems to be ..... 3. His writing is hardly .....

○ **39. intent – to intend**
1. Do you .... to give him more money? 2. He was so .... on finishing his experiment that he did not hear us enter. 3. The criminal looked ....ly at the policeman.

○ **40. intense – intensive**
1. She was overwhelmed with .... emotion. 2. It is ....ly cold. 3. Only .... methods of cultivation can help the farmers in this area.

41. interested – interesting

1. I've just read an .... book. 2. Are you .... in history? 3. Do you find history ....? 4. I met a most .... man yesterday. 5. I'm not .... in meeting Mrs Brown.

42. uninterested – disinterested

1. We must ask a .... party to decide our problem. 2. He is .... in his work. 3. A judge should be .... but he must not be .... .

43. (in)tolerable – (in)tolerant

1. The heat in the room was in.... . 2. He is .... of the views of others. 3. I cannot help considering his words an in.... insolence.

° **44. judicial – judicious**

1. You made a .... decision not to buy that old house. 2. Full faith and credit shall be given in each state to the public acts, records and .... proceedings of every other state *(American Constitution)*. 3. A .... inquiry took place soon after.

° **45. luxurious – luxuriant**

1. They lead a most .... life. 2. They have got a .... house with a .... garden around it. 3. The young man was proud of his .... beard.

° **46. masterful – masterly**

1. The other day we saw a .... performance of the drama in Covent Garden. 2. Melville's Moby Dick is a .... novel. 3. In a .... voice he told us to leave the house.

° **47. momentary – momentous**

1. The peace treaty between the two nations was a .... event. 2. When she saw him smile, she had a .... feeling of happiness. 3. The Watergate scandal was one of the most .... affairs of the Nixon administration.

48. notable – noticeable – noted

1. Carrara is .... for its marble quarries. 2. The difference between the two pictures is easily .... . 3. The landing of the first men on the moon was a .... achievement.

° **49. official – officious**

1. The new clerk is very .... in his duties. 2. The government issued an .... statement. 3. At the airport our luggage was examined by an .... young man.

50. pitiful – pitiable

1. The old woman was .... in her dreadful infirmity. 2. The poor children were in a .... state. 3. The passers-by looked at them ....ly.

° **51. popular – populous**

1. Nigeria is one of the most .... countries in Africa. 2. The headmaster is very .... with his boys. 3. Is baseball .... in Japan?

° **52. potent – potential**

1. Every vessel navigating along a canal is a .... wreck and may be the cause of canal blockage. 2. The newly discovered oil resources are a .... source of wealth to the whole country. 3. The doctor must give him a more .... medicine.

°**53. practical – practicable**

1. The plan seems to be im. . . . . 2. Mr Brown is not very . . . .; he cannot even put up a picture on the wall. 3. They played a . . . . joke on him. 4. Do you think this suggestion . . . . ?

°**54. regretful – regrettable**

1. The accident was due to a . . . . misunderstanding. 2. It is not surprising, however . . . ., that he lost all his money. 3. She was . . . . for what she had done.

55. respectful – respectable

1. They looked at him . . . .ly. 2. Miss Johnson is quite a . . . . person, but her mother always thinks that she is not . . . .ly dressed. 3. Do you think that children ought to be . . . . to their parents?

°**56. rightful – righteous**

1. She is a poor but . . . . woman. 2. Is this house his . . . . property? 3. He is the . . . . heir to a large fortune.

°**57. spiritual – spirituous**

1. How many lords . . . . are there in the House of Lords? 2. A priest is expected to live a . . . . life. 3. '. . . .' means 'containing a lot of alcohol'.

°**58. temporary – temporal**

1. The power of our rulers is only . . . . . 2. He has found . . . . employment only. 3. Has the Pope any . . . . power?

59. triumphant – triumphal

1. Thousands of people were present when the . . . . army marched through the streets of Rome. 2. The emperor himself lead the procession through the . . . . arch.

60. valueless – invaluable

1. His service to the firm has been . . . . . 2. These old stamps are damaged and practically . . . . .

61. various – varied – variable

1. He has had a . . . . life. 2. The weather was . . . . during our holidays. 3. There were . . . . sorts of wines and spirits on the table. 4. Her health is still . . . . . 5. We met . . . . people at the party.

°**62. virtuous – virtual**

1. Mr Harrison is the . . . . manager of the company. 2. She seems to be . . . ., but she is . . . .ly a lady of easy virtue.

63. comic – comical

1. The way he came up the stairs in his wet trousers was rather . . . . . 2. Dickens invented several humorous characters, but you can't call him a . . . . writer. 3. Do you like . . . . strips?

64. economic – economical

1. The increase in oil prices might lead to an . . . . crisis. 2. Such a policy will inflict terrible . . . . damage on the whole country. 3. In future we must be more . . . . in using fuel oil.

○ **65. electric – electrical**
1. Have you got an .... stove or do you cook with gas? 2. Today railways use .... engines. 3. You can buy that sort of plug at an .... supply shop.

○ **66. historic – historical**
1. That problem is of purely .... interest. 2. The .... battlefield of 1066 has ever since borne the name of Battle. 3. When he became Prime Minister in 1940, Churchill made an .... speech.

67. artistic – artificial
1. Esperanto is an .... language. 2. All children were to be begotten by .... insemination *(1984)*. 3. Michelangelo was an .... genius.

79

3. Verbs

Put in the correct words.

a) Cognate Verbs

1. to affect – to effect
1. His invention ....ed many improvements in the manufacturing process. 2. Whatever you do will not .... my decision. 3. The rise in prices ....ed the market.

○ **2. to capture – to captivate**
1. Though they had besieged the town for months, they could not .... it. 2. Soon all the men present were ....ed by her beautiful appearance. 3. Has the thief been ....ed?

3. to convince – to convict
1. The man was ....ed of arson. 2. He could not .... the judge of his innocence. 3. You cannot .... him that he is wrong in this matter.

○ **4. to loose – to loosen**
1. The burglars tried to .... some stones in the wall. 2. The young soldier ....ed the ropes that bound the prisoner, so that he could run away. 3. The new headmaster's ideas ....ed the discipline in the school.

5. to notice – to note
1. When we came home, we ....ed that the door was not locked. 2. Did you .... her leaving the room? 3. Please .... the enclosed directions.

6. to overrun – to run over
1. The car .... a cat. 2. The boy was .... by a taxi. 3. The garden was .... with weeds.

7. to overtake – to take over
1. The road is too narrow here; we can't .... that slow car now. 2. Mr Brown is ill; Mr Green will .... his job for a month. 3. He tried to escape, but his pursuers soon .... him.

○ **8. to overturn – to turn over**
1. The sniper .... the dead body and looked into his brother's face *(Liam O'Flaherty)*. 2. The car skidded on the wet road and ..... 3. The criminal .... a new leaf and became an honest man.

9. to own – to owe

1. She . . . .s her father a lot of money. 2. He . . . .s himself defeated. 3. I . . . . it to you that I'm still alive. 4. He . . . .s a large estate. 5. I still . . . . nearly £200 on my funiture.

10. to suppress – to oppress

1. His mother could not . . . . a sigh when she heard that. 2. There are still countries in which minority groups are mercilessly . . . .ed. 3. I don't believe that the counsel for the defence tried to . . . . evidence.

° **11. to test – to testify**

1. I can . . . . that he was in my house during the time in question. 2. I'm afraid you must have your eyes . . . .ed.

80 **b) Special Forms**

1. born – borne

1. His mother was . . . . in Paris. 2. She has . . . . him four children. 3. He has . . . . the responsibility for years. 4. He is a . . . . sailor. 5. The plane for London was air. . . . at 6.20.

° **2. loaded – laden**

1. The tables were richly . . . . with the most delicious dishes. 2. The cart was . . . . with timber. 3. The old lady seemed to be heavily . . . . with sorrow. 4. Don't open the camera; it's . . . . .

3. past – passed

1. It was half . . . . eight when we . . . . the station. 2. The week has . . . . very quickly. 3. She is always talking about times . . . . . 4. Nothing can bring back the . . . . . 5. What is . . . . is . . . . . 6. Two hours . . . . before she came back.

4. hung – hanged

1. This picture has . . . . here for years. 2. He . . . . himself in his garage. 3. Helen had just . . . . the washing out when it began to rain. 4. The sheriff promised the beggar a lot of money if he . . . . Robin Hood's men.

81 **c) Some Verbs of Special Importance**

1. to lie – to lay

1. Caernarvon . . . . in North Wales. 2. The soldiers . . . . down their arms *(past)*. 3. Where was the key? – It . . . . on the floor. 4. The farmer sells new-. . . . eggs. 5. He will do what . . . . in his power. 6. She . . . . down on the couch *(past)*. 7. She is . . . .ing on the couch now. 8. On Sunday he . . . . in bed until 12 o'clock. 9. I saw an old man . . . .ing on a bench in the park. 10. I'm tired, I must . . . . down for half an hour. 11. Don't . . . . on the bed. 12. Don't . . . . your wet coat on the bed. 13. They are . . . .ing a cable under the river bed. 14. They have . . . . a new cable under the river bed. 15. You should not . . . . too much stress on such points. 16. The man who had been knocked over by the car was . . . . on a stretcher. 17. After he had . . . . there for ten minutes, he was examined by a doctor. 18. We are going to have the floor . . . . with linoleum. 19. Though the garden had been . . . . out by an expert, the owner was dissatisfied. 20. The dead body must have . . . . here for at least three days.

2. to sit – to set *(1. 3. 6. 7. 9. 10. 11.: past tense)*
1. The girl .... the pot on the fire. 2. What time does the sun ....? 3. Last night she .... up till two o'clock in the morning. 4. I'd rather stand than ..... 5. The prisoner was .... free when two thirds of his imprisonment was over. 6. I .... my watch by the station clock. 7. Yesterday he .... over his books for hours. 8. He was accused of ....ing fire to the house. 9. They .... to work as soon as they had arrived. 10. He .... down and began to tell his story. 11. She .... back in her chair and fell asleep. 12. They have just .... out for Canterbury.

3. to rise – to arise – to raise – to rouse – to arouse *(6. 9. 12. 13. 19. 20.: past tense)*
1. They .... their hats when they saw the vicar. 2. Even shaking did not .... him from his deep sleep. 3. She .... herself in her bed so that she could see her baby. 4. He .... when she came into the room. 5. The speaker .... his voice so that everybody could hear him. 6. The government's measures .... general opposition. 7. Soon after they had set sail, a storm ..... 8. New taxes will be .... soon. 9. The rocket .... into the sky. 10. I'm sure it will .... his anger. 11. The men .... their glasses and drank to the greatest benefactor the town had ever had. 12. Bread .... two pence in price. 13. The minister's words .... a lot of criticism. 14. His wages have been .... recently. 15. The price was .... to £20. 16. Prices have .... again recently. 17. He told the boy that he wanted to be .... at seven o'clock. 18. The sun .... at seven. 19. The policeman .... his arm. 20. The fog .... at last. 21. He is a farmer and .... horses. 22. New problems will ..... 23. Has the moon .... yet? 24. The old man was very weak and unable to .....

4. to (a)wake – to (a)waken *(2. 5.: past tense)*
1. My wife .... me at seven every morning. 2. The news .... his suspicion. 3. What time did you ....? 4. What time shall we .... you? 5. When I ...., it was broad daylight. 6. I usually .... at seven.

d) Frequently Confused Verbs 82

1. to arrive – to reach *(1. 2. 3.: past tense)*
1. We .... the airport in time. 2. When we ...., they had just gone out. 3. He .... in Australia some weeks ago. 4. Our goal has been ..... 5. When does the train .... Manchester?

○ **2. to convince – to persuade**
1. I could not .... my father to sell the house. 2. He could not .... the judge of his innocence. 3. At last he succeeded in ....ing her to steal the jewels. 4. She was not ....ed that he had told the truth.

3. to deny – to refuse
1. He ....ed the money offered to him. 2. He ....ed that he had stolen the watch. 3. Her parents .... her nothing she asks for. 4. He ....ed to tell us where he wanted to go. 5. Do you .... that you were in her room last night? 6. He was ....ed a chance to show his abilities. 7. I tried to help her, but was ....ed.

4. to discover – to invent
1. Captain Cook ....ed Hawaii. 2. The telephone was ....ed by Graham Bell. 3. America is said to have been ....ed by Columbus. 4. Who ....ed the steam engine? 5. We were unable to .... who had done it.

5. to rob – to steal *(3. 4. 8. 9.: past tense)*
1. The car in which they escaped was . . . . . 2. Our firm was . . . . last night and a number of things were . . . . . 3. The thief . . . . me of my watch. 4. The thief . . . . my purse. 5. The tourists were . . . . in the mountains of Sardinia. 6. What did you do when you found out that your shop had been . . . . ? 7. £10,000 was . . . . from the bank last night. 8. Burglars . . . . Mrs Blunderstone of all her jewels. 9. Burglars . . . . all her jewels.

6. to take part – to take place
1. What time will the meeting . . . . ? 2. Several good speakers . . . . in the debate. *(past tense)* 3. We had to . . . . in the conference. 4. The wedding will . . . . in three weeks.

83

4. Adverbs

Put in the correct words.

1. first – at first
1. Let's go for a swim . . . .; we can eat afterwards. 2. Open the door for your mother and let her go in . . . . . 3. . . . . I thought he was joking. 4. Who wants to speak . . . . ? 5. . . . . I was not quite sure of his earnestness. 6. . . . . do the kitchen and then make the beds. 7. She was very nervous . . . ., but she soon felt relaxed.

2. last – at last
1. When did you . . . . see him? 2. We lost our way in the forest; . . . . we came to a small hut. 3. He is always the . . . . to come down for breakfast. 4. . . . . he agreed to the proposal. 5. They have come to a decision . . . . . 6. Who is to speak . . . . ? 7. When did you . . . . get a letter from her?

3. at last – at least
1. You ought to take . . . . two tablets a day. 2. Summer seems to have come . . . . . 3. The repairs will cost a lot of money, ... fifty pounds. 4. You've got a lot to do, I know, but you should . . . . be polite.

4. at present – presently
1. . . . . Bob is working in the garden, but he'll come in . . . . . 2. . . . . his parents are on holiday. 3. Mrs Tanner will be back . . . .; she's not at home . . . . .

5. in short – shortly
1. . . . . , you can't have the job. 2. I met him again . . . . afterwards. 3. They will be here . . . . . 4. 'My address,' said Mr Micawber, 'is Windsor Terrace, City Road. I – . . . . ,' said Mr Micawber, 'I live there.' *(Dickens)*

6. sometimes – some time
1. We'll stay here for . . . . . 2. . . . . the postman comes later than usual. 3. I . . . . think I should not help him any longer. 4. I hope I can speak to him about it . . . . in April. 5. That was . . . . ago.

7. always – ever
1. He has . . . . been rather lazy. 2. Have you . . . . been to Scotland? 3. He is . . . . late. 4. If you are . . . . in difficulties, go to your parents. 5. She has been ill . . . . since. 6. I'll remember this day for . . . . . 7. She is . . . . talking about her illnesses. 8. Do you . . . . wish you were a millionaire? 9. I'll come as soon as . . . . I can.

D. Misleading Words ('False Friends')

84

a) *The words in italics are the misleading ones. These words will give the clue to what should go in the gap. (As an additional help the words to be inserted are given below.)*

1. After the shopkeeper had taken the week's takings to the *bank*, he felt so tired that he sat down on a . . . . .
2. Perhaps I'll *become* better at English when we . . . . new and more interesting text books.
3. A soldier must be *brave*, a little boy need not; but if he does not behave well, his mother will say to him, "Try to be a . . . . boy."
4. It is possible to draw a perfect *circle* with a . . . . .
5. Mr A. and Mr F. both teach history at the same *college;* they are . . . .s.
6. As a film *critic* he has his *strong* points; but he is sometimes too . . . . in his . . . . .
7. It is a disgrace that the *floor* of the main . . . . in our school is always covered with waste paper, orange peel and all sorts of litter.
8. The visiting ambassador felt quite *flattered* when he saw his nation's flag . . . .ing in the breeze.
9. The bottle of wine which was a *gift* from his jealous cousin was found to contain . . . . .
10. The *housemaster* wanted to get into the school, but found that it had been locked by the . . . . .

colleague (fellow teacher), (pair of) compass(es), caretaker, flutter, bench, get, severe, poison, good, criticism, corridor

b) *Instructions as for exercise* a)

1. Which is the road to Glencoe? – Wait a moment, I've got a *map* in my . . . . .
2. What's the *meaning* of all this? – In my . . . . there is no sense in it at all.
3. We know how the *murder* was done; all we have to do now is to catch the . . . . .
4. If you never take any *notes*, you can't take part in our discussion. So you can't possibly get good . . . .s.
5. Was Albert Einstein a great *physician?* – No, he was a . . . . .
6. If it wasn't so badly obscured by the *postmark*, this . . . . would be very valuable.
7. My wife is not happy with her new cookery book because it doesn't contain the . . . .s she's interested in. She would like to return it, but she has lost her *receipt*.
8. Do you think a *snake* has a shell on its back? – It hasn't, but a . . . . has.
9. Everybody must *die*, it is true, but it is disgraceful that in some parts of the world there is so little food that people . . . . to death.
10. Every big . . . . is fed by a lot of small *streams*. Among the world's longest . . . .s are the Mississippi, the Amazon and the Nile.
11. You want to be an *undertaker?* – That's possible, of course; I would prefer to be a . . . . of a big company.

mark, recipe, opinion, river, manager, briefcase, stamp, starve, snail, physicist, murderer

c) *Translate the words in italics and put in the missing words.*

1. *The actual profit* of the oil companies was much higher than they had said at the meeting. That is indeed a matter of . . . . interest. *(aktuell)*
2. Lord A. was *a keen advocate* of the preservation of buildings of historic or architectural interest. He is a . . . . by profession. *(Advokat, Anwalt)*

3. Sheila's parents are *too anxious about her well-being*. She is such a shy and .... girl that she will never develop any self-assurance. *(ängstlich)*
4. My aunt likes to visit *art galleries*. – What .... of paintings does she prefer? *(Art)*
5. St Paul's is one of the great *dome-crowned edifices* of Christendom, ranking with the .... of Florence and St Peter's in Rome. *(Dom)*
6. Nylon is *a synthetic fabric*. It is made in a ..... *(Fabrik)*
7. I know her father as *a genial old gentleman*. He is a .... author. *(genial)*
8. The princess gave me *a gracious smile*. She is indeed a charming young lady and a .... dancer. *(graziös)*
9. After *high school* he went to a .... in Wisconsin. *(Hochschule)*
10. Our *landlady* is a ...., who inherited the house from her uncle. *(Landfrau, Bäuerin)*
11. The *magistrate* sentenced the young man to three months' imprisonment for stealing. When his father, who was the treasurer of the ...., heard this, he had a heart attack. *(Magistrat)*
12. Police inspector asking a man whose car was stolen: "Are there *any distinguishing marks on your car?*" – "No, sir, there aren't," – "What .... is it?" – "It's a Ford Consul." *(Marke)*
13. If you have no time *to read a novel* of 400 pages, read some .... by the same author. *(Novellen, Kurzgeschichten)*
14. *I overheard the conversation* in the next room, but I .... some important parts. *(überhörte)*
15. *There is little prospect* of his passing the exam. I'm afraid you'll have to send your son to a private school. I've got some .... here of some schools in the neighbourhood. *(Prospekte)*
16. They have never had *a store of provisions* in the house since their father has been off salary and working on .... only. *(Provision)*
17. I paid the doctor's fee and he sent me a *receipt* together with a new .... for medicine. *(Rezept)*
18. He *took a lot of trouble* over his work, but could not finish it before all the .... caused by his sister's marriage was over. *(Trubel)*
19. We had no time *to wander about* while we were ....ing through Scotland from one youth hostel to the next. *(wandern)*

d) Situational Practice

Mr Walker's Career

Mr Walker had been a .... *(Hausmeister)* at Trinity .... *(Gymnasium)* for more than six years when one day the new headmaster asked him to come into his office. "Walker", he began, "I've just heard that you are unable to read or write. I have the highest .... *(Meinung)* of your character, but we would .... *(uns blamieren)* if we had an illiterate .... *(Hausmeister)* any longer. I'm afraid you'll have to go."

Mr Walker was a very .... *(sensibel)* man and his heart was heavy as he walked along the .... *(Flur)* back to his room. There he put his tea.... *(Kanne)* and some other things in his .... *(Mappe)*, took his coat and .... *(Schal)* and went out into Dulverton .... *(Allee)* where he sat down on a .... *(Bank)*. He did not know what to do. He opened his .... *(Brieftasche)*, there were only a few pounds in it. He had .... *(gespart)* a little money, it is true, but he would not .... *(bekommen)* a .... *(Rente)*. .... *(eventuell)* his .... *(Braut)*, who was a .... *(Schwester)*, could help him to find a job in the hospital.

Then he remembered that he had to buy some .... *(Speck)*, strawberry .... *(Marmelade)* and a .... *(Salat)* on his way home. To his surprise, however, the shop where he used to

do his shopping was closed. As there was no other shop in the street, he had to be content with some bread and butter. – .... *(am anderen Tage)* he suddenly had an idea. 'Why should he not take over the shop and become a grocer himself?'
At first a lot of difficulties had to be overcome. He had to buy everything he needed by .... *(Raten)*. A .... *(Kompagnon)*, who withdrew shortly after, invested only a small sum. During the first months he could hardly .... *(konkurrieren)* with other shops in the neighbourhood, but then, step by step, the number of his customers increased.
Seven years later he was the owner of five supermarkets and a big .... *(Warenhaus)* in the city and was a member of the .... *(Magistrat)*. He had a large bank account and could afford to .... *(spenden)* generously to several charitable organisations.
One day Mr Walker had a talk with the manager of his bank, who advised him to invest some thousand pounds in shares. "We'll do everything for you. All you have to do is to give us your signature." – "Well," replied Mr Walker hesitantly, "the problem is that I can neither write, nor read what I have to sign." The manager jumped up from his chair, "How on earth is it possible that such a .... *(genial)* businessman is unable to read or write? What would you be now if you had been able to?" – Mr Walker answered with a smile: "A .... *(Hausmeister)* at Trinity .... *(Gymnasium)*." *(Based on: W.S. Maugham, The Verger)*

*

On a traffic sign 'SCHOOL ZONE – DON'T KILL A CHILD' somebody added in a .... *(kindlich)* scrawl: "Wait for a teacher."

E. Prepositions

a. Nouns Preceded by Prepositions

1. at, in, on in Expressions of Place **86**

a) at, in *or* on? *Make up suitable sentences.*

I met her ....
I saw it ....

1. .... a party
2. .... the sky
3. .... the wall
4. .... the floor
5. .... the kitchen
6. .... Baker Street
7. .... her wedding
8. .... play
9. .... the hill
10. .... a small island
11. .... Essex
12. .... the Thames
13. .... the butcher's
14. .... Trafalgar Square
15. .... the entrance
16. .... the bus
17. .... Victoria Station
18. .... the picture
19. .... the third floor
20. .... lunch
21. .... Wentworth Street
22. .... the country
23. .... a lecture
24. .... the corner of our street
25. .... the corner of the room
26. .... France
27. .... the cupboard
28. .... her way to school
29. .... the Isle of Skye
30. .... the seaside

31. .... my uncle's farm
32. .... the playground
33. .... the crossroads
34. .... the middle of the road
35. .... the bus stop
36. .... the bottom of the pool
37. .... Manchester
38. .... the mat
39. .... the left-hand side
40. .... the beach
41. .... the end of the queue
42. .... the field

86/87 **b)** *Answer the following questions.*

1. Where's Dad sitting? .... his desk
2. Where does your friend live? .... the country
3. Where are your parents? .... a concert
4. Where do you buy bread? .... the baker's
5. Where's the light switch? .... the wall
6. Where do you see chimneys? .... the roof
7. Where does your father work? .... the General Hospital
8. Where does Mrs Lee buy her vegetables? .... the market
9. Where shall we meet? .... Piccadilly Circus
10. Where do you see plays? .... the theatre
11. Where do you find the number of a page? .... the top
12. Where do you see ducks? .... the lake
13. Where do you see stars? .... the sky
14. Where do you live? .... 10 Chapel Lane
15. Where do you find big stores in London? .... Oxford Street

c) *Put in* at, in *or* on.

1. Please don't sit .... the table. – We were .... table when he came. – He was sitting .... a big table which was full of books and papers. – There were a lot of books .... the table.
2. A man was standing .... the top of the house. – There is a restaurant .... the top of the Post Office Tower in London. – The dictionary must be .... top of that pile of books.
3. What can you see .... the picture? – There are some dirty fingerprints .... this picture. – Who is the man .... the picture?
4. Cows were grazing .... the field. – Farmers must work .... the fields. – The players were practising .... the football field.
5. We like rowing .... the lake. – The town lies .... a lake. In summer we used to swim .... the lake.
6. Her husband works .... a bank. – He works .... the Midland Bank .... London. – He works .... London but lives .... the country. – Two of her sons work .... a farm, the third is .... sea. – She is employed .... the Town Hall. – She is employed .... an office.
7. We spent our holidays .... the coast; .... the seaside; .... a place .... the sea. – We were .... sea for three days. – We saw a lot of ships sailing .... the sea.
8. We live .... a small village. – Shakespeare was born .... Stratford-....-Avon. – My uncle lives .... New York. – My parents live .... Burton.
9. Were you .... church on Sunday? – It was rather cool .... the church. – A fire broke out .... the school. – The children are .... school. – My daughter studies .... a university.
10. Is she .... home? – She is .... the house. – She likes to live .... a bungalow. – We live .... 15 Waterloo Road. – Her mother lives .... a hotel. – She lives .... the Savoy Hotel. – Her sister lives .... her uncle's.
11. The shipwrecked people landed .... a small island; .... Norway; .... Dover; .... the shore.

12. Mountains were to be seen .... the distance. – The noise of the machines can be heard .... a distance of two miles.
13. There were no oranges .... the market yesterday. – We wanted to meet .... the market. – Mother is .... the market this morning. These eggs must be put .... the market as soon as possible.
14. There is a garage .... the side of the house. – There are gardens .... both sides of the road. – Britain fought .... the side of France. – Who is the man standing .... her side?
15. "You smoke fifty cigarettes a day in the office, you say. But aren't you afraid of the ash getting among your letters?"
"Oh, I never smoke .... work."

2. at, in, on in Expressions of Time

a) at, in *or* on? *Make up suitable sentences.* **88**

I met her .... (I'll meet her ....)
I saw it ....

1. .... dinnertime
2. .... half an hour
3. .... Wednesday
4. .... July 24th
5. .... April
6. .... that moment
7. .... noon
8. .... daybreak
9. .... Christmas Day
10. .... Easter
11. .... autumn
12. 1967
13. .... twelve o'clock
14. .... New Year's Day
15. .... a few days
16. .... my wife's birthday
17. .... high tide
18. .... half past six
19. .... Monday
20. .... dusk
21. .... the morning
22. .... September 9th

89

23. .... night
24. .... the morning of Sept. 9th
25. .... the afternoon
26. .... a rainy day in June
27. .... the first evening of our stay in Norfolk
28. .... those days
29. .... Sunday evening
30. .... the appointed time
31. .... that summer morning
32. .... the night
33. .... various occasions
34. .... the same time

b) *Answer the following questions.*

1. When do you hear the clock strike twelve? .... twelve o'clock
2. When do you have tea? .... the afternoon
3. When do you have lunch? .... noon
4. When do you sleep? .... night
5. When do you go to church? .... Sunday
6. When did your grandfather die? .... the age of eighty
7. When is your birthday? .... Oct. 22nd
8. When do children get Easter eggs? .... Easter
9. When do you go for a walk? .... a fine day
10. When must a train arrive? .... time
11. When may we come to see you? .... any time
12. When are you leaving? .... a few days

88/89 **c)** *Put in* at, in *or* on *(where necessary)*.

1. It was early .... the morning. – It was .... the morning of Dec. 25th. – It was .... Christmas. – It was .... Christmas morning. – It was .... the evening of Christmas Day. – It was .... Dec. 25th. – It was .... a Wednesday .... December. – It was .... last Sunday.
2. He will regret doing that .... the end. – My patience is .... an end. – It rained for two days .... end.
3. It happened .... night; .... the afternoon; .... sunset; .... a dark night; .... the night; .... six o'clock; .... Thursday night; .... noon; .... the evening.
4. We reached the station just .... time to catch the train. – It happened .... the wrong time. – He always gets to work .... time.

86/89 *Put in* at, in *or* on.

1. My Name is Sheila Williams. I live .... 25 Randolph Crescent .... Bexhill, a small town .... the sea. Our house is .... a railway line .... the foot of the hill. .... the distance we can see the sea. My father works .... the Cavendish Hotel; my mother is employed .... a shop.
2. .... weekdays I get up .... half past seven .... the morning. I help my mother put the cups and plates .... the table. We have breakfast .... eight. .... summer I ride to school .... my bike .... fifteen minutes. .... cold days .... winter I take the bus to get to school .... time. .... the evening I am .... home again .... five o'clock.
3. There is no school .... Saturdays and Sundays. We spend the weekends .... our garden, ... the seaside, ... the country, ... my uncle's farm or sailing .... a lake.

90

3. Other Frequently Confused Prepositions

Put in the correct prepositions.

a) after – behind
1. I ran .... the boy but could not catch him. 2. It is dangerous to run .... a bus. 3. The dog used to run .... his master's bicycle. 4. Do you think the police are .... him?

b) ago – before
1. We last saw him two years ....; he had retired from business six months ..... 2. Two weeks .... I was in London; the week .... I had been in Bristol. 3. I told you a week .... that I had given the money back to him a fortnight .....

c) between – among
1. The profits were divided .... the two partners. 2. He fell .... thieves. 3. I sat .... an elderly lady and a young, fair-haired girl. 4. He knew that there was a detective .... the tourists. 5. The rum was distributed .... the crew. 6. The treaty .... the three powers will be signed in April. 7. The children hid .... the bushes. 8. Switzerland lies .... Germany, Austria, Italy and France. 9. We were not at home .... four and six in the afternoon.

d) except (but) – besides – beside
1. She was .... herself with anxiety. 2. They all went .... him. 3. I didn't want to go out; ...., it was raining. 4. There were no applicants .... him. 5. There were three applicants .... him. 6. If you sit .... me, we can have a quiet chat. 7. The shops are open every day .... Sunday. 8. I've got two other coats .... this one. 9. All the tables were occupied .... the

one at the entrance. 10. .... our table two others were occupied. 11. All the countries agreed .... France. 12. The boy wanted to sit .... the driver.

e) for – since

1. He came to Manchester in 1962 and has been here ever ..... 2. We have been learning English .... September; so we have been studying it .... six months. 3. We lived in Edinburgh .... ten years; .... then we have been living here in Aberdeen. 4. I haven't seen her .... our schooldays. 5. How long have you been married? – .... five years; .... 1969. 6. There has been no rain here .... July. 7. I haven't seen him .... ages. 8. It is about twelve years .... I saw him. 9. Things have changed a lot .... the last time I saw you. 10. It has been raining .... days. 11. No buses have been running .... the strike began. 12. She slept .... nine hours last night.

f) by – in – on – with

1. It is pleasant to ride .... his new car. 2. Next year we will make a tour of Scotland .... coach or .... car. 3. He tried to open the bottle .... a screwdriver. 4. Has he come .... horseback? – No, ... foot. 5. The door was opened .... the thieves .... a skeleton key. 6. He rides to school .... his bicycle. 7. He comes to school .... bicycle. 8. These goods are made .... machinery, not .... hand. 9. The thief got away .... a taxi. 10. I paid the bill .... cheque. 11. Do you go there .... train or .... bus? 12. When you were a boy, Grandfather, was the street lit .... electricity? 13. The easiest way to get from one station to the other is to go .... taxi. 14. In the end I managed to beat the dog off .... a stick. 15. In former times this mill was driven .... water. 16. It will be quicker to send it .... air than .... rail.

g) to – as far as

1. We went .... Chester, then on by bus .... Hoylake. 2. As there was no inn or hotel in the village, we went on .... the nearest town. 3. The bus goes only .... the station. 4. You can get from here .... London in about two hours. 5. Read .... line eight.

h) till (until) – by

1. I promised to have the work finished .... Friday. 2. We must wait .... six o'clock. 3. He should have been here .... now. 4. .... her marriage she worked as a shop assistant. 5. We had to work .... six o'clock. 6. I'll be back .... 4 o'clock. 7. Office hours are from eight .... four o'clock. 8. The patient had felt quite well .... Sunday; on Monday he got worse. 9. I hope we'll reach Winchester .... 5; but if there's a lot of traffic, we'll have to be on the road .... 7.

i) over – across – above – via (by)

1. We flew .... the clouds. 2. Can you swim .... the river? 3. The boys always kick the ball .... the wall. 4. The tower can be seen .... the trees. 5. The shop is just .... the street. 6. The plane flew .... the town. 7. The maid spread the cloth .... the table. 8. As we could not open the gate, we climbed .... it. 9. His income is .... the average. 10. A tree had fallen .... the railway line. 11. We went to the Channel Islands .... Southampton. 12. The kettle must hang .... the fire.

j) under – below

1. His leg was broken .... the knee. 2. The thief crept .... the bed. 3. The boat passed .... the bridge. 4. From the top of the mountain we could see the other men far .... us. 5. It's rather cold. I'm afraid it's .... zero. 6. During the rain we were standing .... a tree. 7. Sign your name .... mine on this document.

k) at – by – in – on

.... no account; .... any case; .... no means; .... all events; .... no case; .... any rate; .... all means

l) Just for Fun

1. During the night a farmer heard a noise in the chicken coop. With a gun in his hand he flung the door wide open and shouted: "Come out of there, you thief!" – A faltering voice answered: "There's nobody here .... *(außer)* us chickens."

2. The conductor of a bus had some difficulty with small change. When a woman with a baby on her arm handed him a ten-pound note, he asked her: "Is that the smallest you have, madam?" The woman looked at the conductor and then at the baby and answered: "Yes, I have been married only .... *(seit)* one year."

91

4. Nouns of Similar Meaning Preceded by the Same Preposition

at, by, for, in, on or ....? *Put in the correct prepositions.*

1. I learned the verses .... heart .... no particular reason.
2. .... average the train travels .... a speed of 90 mph.
3. Side .... side they went back .... the direction of the hotel.
4. .... my opinion the metal will melt .... a temperature of 2000°C.
5. If they want to climb the mountain .... this rainy weather, they'll do it .... their own risk.
6. She paused .... the sound of his voice .... fear of annoying him.
7. What did you say .... answer .... her question? – I told her that I had done it .... purpose.
8. .... the way, I met him .... chance yesterday, but I was .... such a hurry that I couldn't have a talk with him.
9. .... all probability we won't get home before midnight if we go on driving .... this rate.
10. .... this way he has been living for years .... his brother's expense.
11. .... my sake, say it .... English.
12. He said .... a loud voice that he had bought the flowers .... 50p a dozen.
13. He ought to be .... duty from twelve to six. .... my watch it is a quarter past six already.
14. Lieutenant Smith is .... leave in London. .... order ..... the Captain he is to be back on board by 3 p.m.
15. He is a baker .... trade. Day .... day he must get up at 5.
16. Is your partner .... holiday? – No, he is in Glasgow .... business. He had to go to Scotland .... the request of some customers.
17. Are you going to do that .... fun? – .... the contrary, it's hard work and I'm doing it .... one condition only: that I can make a nice profit out of it.
18. John is a good-humoured fellow .... nature; .... the whole, he has been a good friend.
19. As they were unable to break the door open .... force, the burglars entered the house .... means .... a ladder.
20. .... want of money they bought the furniture .... instalments.
21. .... this purpose detailed instructions will be delivered to customers .... request free of charge.

b. Verbs and Adjectives Followed by Prepositions

1. Words Followed by Different Prepositions

Put in the correct prepositions (if necessary).

a) Verbs **92**

1. admit 1. The caretaker will admit you .... the building. 2. About 120 boys and girls are admitted .... our school every year. 3. You can be sure to be admitted .... the club.

2. agree 1. I hope she will agree .... my plan. 2. They could not agree .... the price. 3. The wine does not agree .... me. 4. I agree .... you .... this point. 5. We agreed .... one respect only. 6. Her father agreed .... her studying medicine. 7. Do you agree .... me that it was his fault? 8. They all agreed .... considering August the best time for a holiday in Scotland.

3. apply 1. If you want to be admitted into the club, you must apply .... the secretary. 2. If you want to apply .... admission, go to the secretary. 3. He applied .... his employer .... a loan.

4. arrive 1. He arrived .... New York before I did. 2. When will we arrive .... our destination? 3. I usually arrive .... school about five minutes to nine. 4. The tourists arrived .... Japan early in the morning.

5. ask 1. The beggar asked the passers-by .... money. 2. Mrs Brown asked .... you when I met her yesterday. 3. She asked .... him to help her. 4. We went to the station to ask .... the trains. 5. He asked .... me how to open the suitcase. 6. Her old father is ill; did you ask .... his health? 7. If you want to apply for the post, ask .... Mr Atwood.

6. blush 1. The young lady blushed .... the dirty joke. 2. The boy blushed .... his mistake. 3. When she was told that she had failed in the examination, she blushed .... embarrassment.

7. call 1. I called .... her at 8 o'clock, but she was not yet ready to leave. 2. I called .... his house some time ago. 3. Perhaps I'll call .... him again tomorrow. 4. The wounded soldier called .... some water. 5. Please call me .... in the evening. 6. These crimes call .... punishment. 7. I'll call .... him .... his house and we'll go for a walk together.

8. care 1. She should take care .... her old parents. 2. She should care .... her old parents. 3. Bernard doesn't care .... wine. 4. My brother doesn't care .... other people's difficulties. 5. Would you care .... a drink? 6. He is very much interested in foreign countries, but she doesn't care .... travelling.

9. change 1. Our neighbour has changed his old car .... a new one. 2. The conjuror changed the scarf .... a white pigeon. 3. The customer asked the shop assistant if she could change the yellow pullover .... a red one. 4. Where do I change .... Oxford?

10. charge 1. The officer was charged .... treason. 2. This is a nice hotel; I wonder what they charge .... a room. 3. The police inspector is charged .... further investigations in the case. 4. How much did they charge you .... repairing the car? 5. The boy is charged .... stealing.

11. come 1. The other day I came .... an old friend on the bus. 2. It came .... just as he had told us. 3. The laundry man has come .... the shirts. 4. Turning out some papers from her desk, she came .... an envelope with pictures of her parents.

12. compare 1. The heart is often compared .... a pump. 2. The teacher compared my paper .... John's. 3. Her lover compared her eyes .... pearls. 4. "Shall I compare thee .... a summer's day?" *(Shakespeare)* 5. It is impossible to compare the two poems .... each other.

13. complain 1. What have you got to complain ....? 2. She is always complaining .... her son .... her daughter-in-law. 3. You'd better complain .... the manager himself. 4. He complained .... a headache.

14. condemn 1. He was condemned .... treason. 2. They condemned him .... death. 3. I'm sure he'll be condemned .... imprisonment .... his crime.

15. consist, insist, persist 1. His success as a lawyer consists .... his outstanding power of persuasion. 2. She insisted .... getting a single-berth cabin. 3. A baseball team consists .... nine players. 4. He persists .... his silly idea. 5. The drink consists .... gin and lemon juice. 6. The citizens insisted .... their rights. 7. Does the old man still persist .... living quite alone in the house?

16. deal 1. I hope I'll never have to deal .... her mother. 2. My friend deals .... wool. 3. This chapter deals .... the National Health Service. 4. We'll never again deal .... such a firm. 5. The village store deals .... goods of all sorts.

17. delight(ed) 1. The children were delighted .... their Christmas presents. 2. The children were delighted .... finding their presents under the Christmas tree. 3. The old man delights .... telling stories about his youth. 4. Her parents were delighted .... the result of her work. 5. She takes great delight .... playing the piano.

18. die 1. His mother died .... an incurable disease. 2. He died .... his own hands. 3. A lot of people die .... hunger every year. 4. He died .... his family. 5. Nelson died .... a wound.

19. distinguish 1. The twins are so much alike that it is difficult to distinguish one .... the other. 2. Can their parents distinguish .... them? – Yes, certainly. 3. Mr Patterson distinguished himself .... his far-sighted management of the company. 4. He cannot distinguish Scotch whisky .... Bourbon. 5. St Bernard dogs are distinguished .... their intelligence. 6. Death does not distinguish .... the rich and the poor.

20. divide 1. Can you divide 17 .... 3? 2. His money was divided .... his two daughters. 3. His money was divided .... his five daughters. 4. Divide the melon .... halves. 5. Divide it .... four parts.

21. give 1. More and more people are giving .... smoking. 2. After a long dispute neither of the two business partners would give .... . 3. Mothers should not always give .... to their children. 4. Seeing that he had no chance to win the race, he gave .... .

22. hear 1. Have your ever heard .... John Webster, an Elizabethan dramatist? 2. I hope to hear .... you soon. 3. We were all shocked when we heard .... the accident. 4. I have often heard .... your daughter. – How? – .... our neighbour.

23. hope 1. There is no hope .... saving her life. 2. There is nothing to hope .... any longer. 3. She has hoped .... her recovery for months. 4. She lost all hope .... her recovery.

24. inquire 1. I inquired .... his health, but he did not say a word. 2. I inquired .... his wife if he was seriously ill. 3. He went to inquire .... a letter at the post office. 4. She inquired .... her sister .... the matter.

25. introduce 1. I'll introduce you .... her mother. 2. A new consideration was introduced .... the discussion. 3. Will you please introduce me .... Sir John? 4. A new history book has lately been introduced .... the school.

26. judge 1. Judging .... what you say about him, he will suit the post. 2. It is difficult to judge .... the general style of the building .... such a bad picture. 3. Things present are judged .... things past.

27. lean 1. The old man was leaning .... a stick. 2. You can lean .... my arm. 3. Don't lean .... the door, it is still wet with paint.

28. live 1. She lives .... her friend. 2. He lives .... bread and butter only. 3. The blind man lives .... making baskets. 4. He earns scarcely enough to live ..... 5. My parents live .... 77 Garden Lane.

29. look 1. She looks .... me as her best friend. 2. If you cannot find the article in the encyclopedia, look it .... in the index. 3. Look ....! A car is coming. 4. The burglar looked .... him before he broke the lock. 5. He is so proud of his success that he looks .... all his former friends. 6. Can the girl look .... her little sister? 7. We are looking .... our holiday abroad. 8. It took me several hours to look .... the report. 9. You should look .... it that such a thing will never happen again. 10. He's not taking part in the game, he's merely looking ..... 11. I just wanted to look .... and see if you were all right again. 12. The mayor of our town is the kind of man people look .... 13. Why are you looking .... me like that? 14. The police promised to look .... the case again. 15. Ask your teacher to look .... your letter of application before you post it. 16. Grandma is always looking .... her glasses.

30. pity 1. His wife took pity .... the poor woman. 2. She felt pity .... the helpless child. 3. We had pity .... the young man.

31. point 1. He pointed .... that there was little chance of success. 2. It is rude to point .... people. 3. Before I had seen the tiger, my companion had already pointed his rifle .... him. 4. His speech pointed .... some common abuses.

32. speak 1. The boys were speaking .... cars. 2. The teacher often asked the girls to speak ..... 3. He often met her on the bus, but did not dare to speak .... her. 4. The parents spoke .... spending the weekend at the seaside. 5. My friend never speaks .... his first wife. 6. Dr Clarke will speak .... "Improvements in Microelectronic Technology". 7. We were speaking .... different subjects. 8. He spoke .... a doctor .... his problems.

33. stay 1. My aunt stayed .... us for two weeks. 2. Yesterday they stayed .... till two o'clock in the morning. 3. John is ill; he must stay .... for some days. 4. Why did her husband stay .... for such a long time?

34. take 1. What do you take me ....? 2. After he had come in, he took .... his hat and coat. 3. He took her .... the arm and led her out of the room. 4. In America I was taken .... an Englishman.

35. think 1. I'll think .... your proposal. 2. We had thought .... a holiday in Florida, but as we didn't have much money, we couldn't go. 3. She thinks too much .... her illnesses.

36. turn 1. Though he had never been in the mountains before, he turned .... an excellent mountaineer. 2. A caterpillar turns .... a butterfly. 3. In his deperate situation he turned .... all his friends for help. 4. The day turned .... to be a very successful one.

37. wait 1. When he is ill, he likes to be waited .... by his children. 2. I've been waiting .... you since 12 o'clock. 3. We can't go up the mountain today; we must wait .... better weather. 4. Two nice girls waited .... us at dinner.

38. weep 1. The injured man wept .... pain. 2. The women wept .... the death of the children. 3. She wept .... the sad news. 4. He left his wife five years ago; why should she now weep .... him in his misfortune?

39. write 1. What is written .... ink is clearer than what is written .... pencil. 2. I wrote a letter .... my friend in Manchester yesterday. 3. Who shall I write .... first? 4. What shall I write ....? 5. I cannot write .... this pen.

Just for Fun

1. A farmer complained .... a dentist that seven dollars was far too much to pull out a tooth – a job which takes just a few seconds.
The dentist replied: "Well, if you prefer, I can pull it very slowly."

2. Teacher: "If I take a potato and divide it .... halves and split the two parts .... four parts and the four parts .... eight parts, what will I have?"
Alan: "You'll have potato salad."

93 **b) Adjectives and Participles**

1. angry (annoyed) 1. She was very angry .... what he had done. 2. Please don't be angry .... me. 3. Your father is very annoyed .... you. 4. He got annoyed .... your remark.

2. anxious 1. He is anxious .... his son's absence. 2. Lady S. was anxious .... her daughter to be engaged to Lord M. 3. We were anxious .... news of her safe arrival.

3. blind 1. He is blind .... her faults. 2. His wife was blind .... jealousy. 3. The horse was blind .... one eye. 4. Blind .... fury he broke the door open.

4. (in)dependent 1. Children like to be independent .... their parents. 2. All our plans will remain dependent .... the weather. 3. Judges must be independent .... political pressure. 4. We can depend .... him for assistance.

5. desirous, desire 1. After the long march we all had a great desire .... rest. 2. I'm not desirous .... seeing her again. 3. He does not work hard and has no desire .... wealth.

6. engaged 1. Bernard is engaged .... my sister. 2. Father is engaged .... repairing his car. 3. The Smiths are engaged .... planning their summer holiday.

7. familiar 1. I'm not familiar .... that subject. 2. Are you familiar .... the works of Thornton Wilder? 3. That song is familiar .... every Englishman.

8. made 1. Cider is made .... apples. 2. The salad we had was made .... cucumber, lettuce and tomatoes. 3. What sort of wood is that box made ....? 4. Flour is made .... wheat. 5. Her dress was made .... the finest velvet.

9. proud, etc. 1. He takes a lot of pride .... his work. 2. Mary is proud .... her five sons. 3. She prides herself .... her five sons. 4. Is that the car he is so proud ....?

10. tired 1. We were tired .... climbing the hill. 2. He is tired .... listening to her silly stories. 3. We are tired .... having the same food every day.

2. Words of Similar Meaning Followed by the Same Preposition

94

Put in suitable prepositions.

a) at – for – of – to?

1. The burglar aimed his pistol .... me. He fired .... me but missed.
2. After the long period of rain we longed .... sunshine.
3. Who did you address the letter ....?
4. She accused him .... cheating her.
5. The ship has just set sail .... Jersey.
6. Do people still bow .... the Queen?
7. He was too proud to appeal .... his friends .... help.
8. It is rude to point .... people.
9. The child fixedly gazed .... the funny hat of the lady opposite her.
10. Yesterday he departed .... Scotland.
11. After a long investigation he was acquitted .... theft because the evidence against him was not strong enough.
12. Does she often write .... you?
13. What are you waiting ....?
14. Why are you looking .... me like that?
15. She has hoped .... her recovery for months.
16. The beggar asked the passers-by .... money.
17. Have you replied .... her letter in the meantime?
18. Don't throw stones .... the birds. – Throw the ball .... your little sister.
19. The ship is bound .... Bombay.
20. In his speech the candidate alluded .... some weak points in his opponent's career.
21. I'm afraid we must send .... the doctor.
22. I can't pay .... this furniture now.
23. The officer glanced .... my passport without much care.
24. The young man applied .... his employer .... a loan.
25. We are going to embark .... Australia next week.
26. The little boy was staring .... the toys in the shop window.
27. Are you still looking .... a job?
28. The speaker should confine himself .... the essential points.
29. .... my question concerning his income, he answered that at the moment he had no income at all.
30. Why are they opening all the suitcases? What are they looking ....?
31. This book is very expensive; so the edition was limited .... 2,000 copies.

b) at – for – from – with?

1. He fell in love .... her .... a party.
2. We must try to preserve these documents .... harm.
3. I hate myself .... having done that.
4. Everybody wondered .... the man's courage.
5. I hope Pat is pleased .... her birthday presents.
6. Soldiers helped to rescue the villagers .... the flood.
7. The officer was reproached .... dishonesty.
8. The people in the theatre were struck .... panic when they saw that the curtain had caught fire.

9. What are you laughing ....?
10. What have you done to secure your house .... burglars?
11. She was beside herself .... anger.
12. The woman wept .... the sad news.
13. Why do you always find fault .... your brother?
14. Defend us .... all perils and dangers of this night.
15. The girls mocked .... the boy's ignorance.
16. The boy shouted .... joy .... the sight of his new bicycle.
17. We all rejoiced .... your good fortune.
18. The poor children were shivering .... cold.
19. The teacher smiled .... the girl's funny explanation.
20. There was not even a tree to shelter us .... the rain.
21. He was praised .... his energy and courage.
22. Halfway up the mountain she fainted .... exhaustion.
23. Don't grumble .... everything.
24. I'm afraid we'll have to put up .... this situation.
25. The future is hidden .... us.
26. He was blamed .... his laziness.
27. The boy saved their friend .... drowning.
28. Keep us .... harm and protect us .... our enemies.
29. The young lady blushed .... the dirty joke.
30. When he was told that he had failed in the examination, he blushed .... embarrassment.
31. She tried to conceal the letter .... her husband.
32. Can't you see that the little girl is trembling .... fear?
33. Her parents were delighted .... the result of her work.
34. The old man shuddered .... the thought of the air raid during which his wife was killed.
35. We can't punish him .... that; he is innocent.

c) in – into – of – on?

1. The old people despaired .... ever seeing their son again.
2. Are you interested .... modern music?
3. I'm sure we can count .... him for support.
4. Can you translate the sentence .... French?
5. The ambassador was engaged .... sorting out some important documents.
6. He assured us .... the truth of his assertion.
7. I must rely .... the train arriving on time.
8. Trust .... God, and you need not be afraid .... anything.
9. Do you know .... anyone who can help me write a letter in Spanish?
10. Dick hasn't joined .... our games since he fell ill.
11. She soon repented .... having offended him.
12. My son is very keen .... soccer.
13. Do you believe .... God?
14. I was thinking .... Brian when in he came.
15. A caterpillar turns .... a butterfly.
16. He should not always boast .... his achievements.
17. My friend succeeded .... getting the job he had applied for.
18. She spends a lot of money .... cigarettes.
19. Did you take part .... the meeting?
20. Do you know how to put that .... English?

21. The fact that he inherited a lot of money had no effect .... his moral attitude.
22. The old man delights .... telling stories about his youth.
23. We often speak .... her and think .... her.
24. Three brothers shared .... the use of the car.
25. Is he convinced .... the truth of the report?
26. He has always had a bad influence .... his younger brother.
27. The village store deals .... goods of all sorts.
28. He failed .... his attempt to climb the mountain.
29. The conjuror changed the scarf .... a white pigeon.
30. A policeman informed the old lady .... the death of her husband.
31. You may depend .... me.
32. Why do so many people dream .... a white Christmas?

d) by – from – to?

1. Mr Prendergast retired .... business at the age of 65.
2. Has he recovered .... his illness?
3. He took her .... the hand and led her out of the room.
4. Are you really going to marry your daughter .... such a man?
5. May I conclude .... this hint that in your opinion he is an impostor?
6. The plate fell .... the ground and broke .... pieces.
7. The robber bound the owners of the house .... their iron bedstead.
8. The cowboy was leading his horse .... the bridle when he entered the camp.
9. Judging .... what you say about him, he will suit the post.
10. After the storm we had to remove a lot of twigs and some branches .... the garden path.
11. I'm far .... blaming you for it.
12. Don't stick .... those old customs.
13. Three men escaped .... prison last night.
14. The rain kept us .... going for a walk.
15. The old lady tied her dog .... a chair.
16. His parents tried to prevent him .... marrying that woman.
17. At the airport labels were attached .... our luggage.
18. Deliver us .... evil.
19. I'll never get accustomed .... this wet climate.
20. During the war the children were separated .... their parents.
21. The policeman caught the thief .... the collar.
22. I've been suffering .... a bad cold for two weeks.
23. His daughter is married .... the American ambassador in Paris.
24. The village is about 30 miles .... the nearest town.
25. In what respect does your opinion differ .... your brother's?
26. Keep away .... the boss while he is so angry.
27. The shipwrecked people clung .... some logs and casks.
28. The accident resulted .... negligence.
29. The robber seized me .... the arm but I was able to escape.
30. After five years he was released .... prison.
31. About ten different posters were fastened .... the wall with pins.
32. Can you distinguish a lion .... a tiger?

e) at – for – of – with?

1. Everybody was astonished .... what he had done.
2. I dare say she was surprised .... his decision.

3. The accused was found guilty .... murder.
4. Lady S. was anxious .... her daughter to be married to Lord M.
5. The girl was ill .... measles.
6. I'm hungry .... a good steak.
7. Miss Armstrong is happy .... her new position.
8. I was alarmed .... his behaviour.
9. We are fond .... swimming.
10. He is very proud .... his new car.
11. The streets were wet .... rain when the accident happened.
12. She is greedy .... money.
13. The old lady was glad .... a rest after the long walk.
14. We were shocked .... the sight of the dead man.
15. I'm eager .... an opportunity to give him a piece of my mind.
16. The children were delighted .... finding their presents under the Christmas tree.
17. He does not work hard and has no desire .... wealth.
18. I'm tired .... listening to your silly ideas.
19. On hearing that, he went pale .... anger.
20. I'm amazed .... your forgetfulness.
21. He was stiff .... cold when they found him in the snow.
22. The jury came to the decision that the man was innocent .... the crime he was accused .....
23. How can you be afraid .... such a small dog?
24. He got angry .... her remark.
25. Is he conscious .... his guilt?
26. A mother's love .... her children will never end.
27. We were tired .... climbing the hill.
28. Mr Callaghan has a preference .... his youngest niece.
29. She has always been jealous .... her younger sister.
30. I'm not sure .... the time of arrival.
31. My wife is afraid .... spiders.
32. Hastings is known .... the famous battle of 1066 which was fought near the town.
33. The boss was furious .... the clerk's negligence.
34. Oxford and Cambridge are famous .... their old colleges.
35. He seems to be ignorant .... the simplest rules of grammar.
36. He was mad .... fury when he heard that.
37. North Wales is noted .... its old castles.
38. The old lady was grieved .... the death of her dog.
39. Aren't you ashamed .... your laziness?

f) at – in – of – to?

1. The boys are no good .... cricket at all.
2. The bed of the North Sea is rich .... oil.
3. I'm most grateful .... him for all he has done for me.
4. There is an abundance .... apples this year.
5. A lot of accidents arise from lack .... care.
6. It is very useful .... me to have a craftsman as a neighbour.
7. His proposal shows a poverty .... ideas.
8. She does not do her work very carefully; besides, she is very slow .... it.
9. My grandfather was faithful .... his principles throughout his life.

10. Thousands of people die from lack .... food every year.
11. That lake is abundant .... fish.
12. The little girl is clever .... puzzles.
13. The boy is not wanting .... intelligence.
14. John, please, be so kind as to be a little more polite .... Aunt Lily.
15. The officer was deaf .... the soldiers' complaints.
16. The manager is still young .... years.
17. He is quite blind .... her faults.
18. The farmer seems to be cruel .... his dog.
19. The boy is quick .... figures.
20. The patient is lacking .... energy; so you can't be sure .... his recovery.
21. You should be kind .... your parents.
22. Your report will be very useful .... me.
23. The girls is weak .... mathematics but very good .... English.
24. Smoking is dangerous .... health.
25. The Scottish Highlands are poor .... forests and agricultural land.
26. The court decision was advantageous .... the plaintiff.
27. What he said was most interesting .... all of us.

Situational Practice (Prepositions) **86-94**

Put in suitable prepositions.

1. How is Sheila getting on .... school? – Oh, she's getting on fine .... *(außer)* .... Maths; she's rather bad .... Maths, I'm afraid she isn't interested .... it .... all. She's good .... languages, however. She spends two hours or more .... French every day. .... the moment she's looking forward .... a stay .... France next month. – How does she get .... school? – That depends .... the weather. .... rainy weather she goes .... bus, ... fine days she goes .... foot.

2. There was a foreigner .... *(unter)* the guests who wanted to buy the picture that hung .... the wall .... any price. He said that he dealt .... pictures and would pay .... it .... once. .... the end the owner could not help giving .... .

3. John is always .... a hurry. He always drives .... a tremendous speed. .... midnight .... October 1st he had an accident .... a wet road, but he succeeded .... getting .... the burning car. He was taken .... hospital at once. Now he has been .... hospital .... four weeks and is still suffering .... his burns.

4. The sailor fastened his boat .... the quay and went .... the nearest house. He leant .... the wall and waited .... the smugglers. He was shivering .... cold and tired .... waiting when a policeman seized him .... the collar.

5. About five years .... Dick fell .... love .... her .... a party. Now he has been engaged .... her .... six months. They are going to marry .... Easter, ... all probability .... Easter Monday.

6. When we were .... holiday last year, my friend and I wanted to dine .... a restaurant which was famous .... its big steaks. We had lived .... tinned food .... days. We had to search .... the restaurant and, when we arrived .... last, we were astonished .... the shabbiness .... the furniture. We were waited .... a stout young man, who, judging .... the way he laid the table, was a woodcutter .... trade.

7. Eager .... a good steak as we were, we were ready to put up .... everything, though I was a little angry .... my friend .... having suggested going there. When the waiter brought the steaks, we looked .... each other .... surprise. The steaks were far .... big; .... the contrary, they were the smallest we had ever seen. .... top of that they were so tough that we were glad they were so small. – The restaurant we had been .... search .... was next door!

8. .... my opinion Mrs Jones is not too old to look .... a job. When she married .... the age .... 25, she had given .... a good position .... a department store. Now that the children were no longer .... home, she was eager .... some diversion and thought .... applying .... a part-time job. .... course her husband was not pleased .... the idea, but she insisted .... doing something and convinced him .... the advantages; .... a little extra money they would be able to pay .... the new furniture and the car they were dreaming .... . So, ... last, he agreed .... her plan.

9. Some days later she came .... an advertisement for a job that seemed to be agreeable .... her. A home .... animals that took care .... dogs, cats, birds and other pets while their masters were .... holiday or .... work was .... need .... a helper. As Mrs Jones was very fond .... animals, she made .... her mind to apply .... the lady who was .... charge .... the home. Yesterday she told me that she had succeeded .... getting the job.

10. .... Saturday last I was invited .... a party. When I arrived .... the house, Mr Hennerley was already waiting .... me on the veranda. He introduced me .... the other guests and I apologized .... being late. A fair-haired young lady smiled .... me, and I was just .... the point .... heading .... a vacant seat .... her side when Mrs Hennerley asked me to sit next .... Mrs Pilkington .... the sofa. I was beside myself .... anger, for now nobody would be able to preserve me .... the talkativeness of the old lady. First .... all she informed me .... her various illnesses, and all that .... a loud voice, then she began to boast .... her grandchildren.

11. I am not used .... listening .... anybody without having a chance .... saying a word. Nobody had pity .... me when Mrs Pilkington complained .... the rising prices and told me .... her stay .... Iowa, where she had lived .... her sister .... some months. I was not released .... her until her husband, who had been .... London .... business, called .... her.

12. "Good-bye, dear", said he, rising from the breakfast table, "and if I'm prevented .... coming home this evening, I'll send you a note."
"Thank you very much," she replied, "I've already taken it out of your letter case."

90.12.35/25***